P[illegible]

Max Freedom Long called **Huna** a "psycho-religious" [illegible] because it contains elements of both psychology and religion. As psychology, it is practical and effective; as religion it is a simple, yet complete Way of Life. In addition to the basic texts written during Max Freedom Long's fifty years of research and experimentation with Huna, there is a growing number of important books written by Huna students and practitioners. The students have the advantage of all of MFL's writings as well as their own experiences, and their insights add to our understanding and ability to use Huna effectively.

William R. "Bill" Glover, a builder of yachts in southern California, had investigated the religious beliefs of the many countries he had visited in his wide travels. His quest for a reasonable philosophy of life led him to an interest in the writings of Max Freedom Long. Using Max's taped lectures, Bill began to rework them for presentation to his classes on positive thinking.

"When I found I didn't get a point across very well," he said, "I modified the talk and then used the new lecture on the next group. So actually these lectures are the result of a number of re-writes." He began to correlate current beliefs with the ancient thought of the Kahuna, and this book is the result.

It is significant to point out that Max Freedom Long had an opportunity to examine the revised lectures and found them excellent, especially for introducing Huna to new students. He encouraged their publication. The first printing won ready acceptance. We are pleased to offer this fourth printing in a new format.

After reading this fascinating introduction to the **Huna approach to creative prayer,** examine the Bibliography for suggestions for further study.

October, 1983

Dr. E. Otha Wingo, Director
Huna Research, Inc.

INTRODUCTION

Huna: *The Ancient Religion of Positive Thinking* presents in logical steps the basic concepts of an ancient secret system of "Positive Thinking" which has been traced back to early Egypt. This system, which eventually spread throughout the world, has influenced the basic beliefs of all modern religions. Unfortunately outside influences ultimately contaminated the original beliefs and the system became lost. However, many of the concepts were preserved in the remote islands of Polynesia and have been recovered, in part, during the past century.

Huna, which means "secret," teaches that man is composed of three separate and independent units of consciousness which make use of the physical body during life. This belief correlates nicely with modern psychology's subconscious mind, conscious mind and superconscious mind.

Each "mind" uses a basic "life force" for a specific purpose. Proper utilization of this energy, plus the Huna techniques of creative prayer, can create success for every reader, whether measured in terms of money, power, health, or peace of mind.

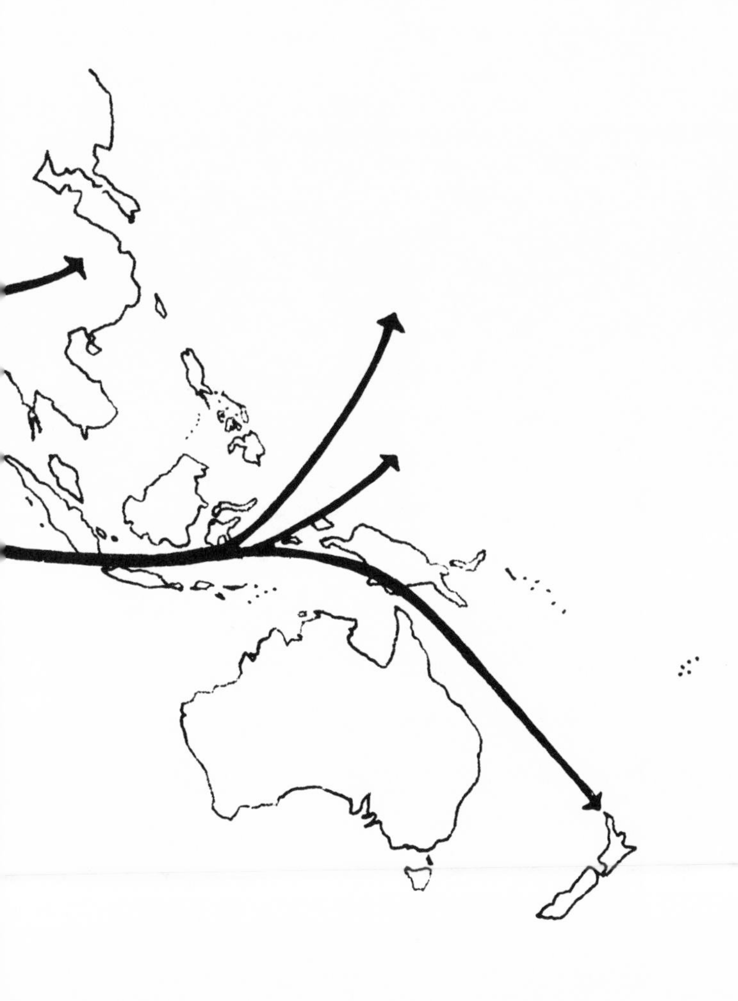

The purpose of this book is to teach the reader the simple techniques of creative prayer. Parallels are shown between these ancient techniques and the more scientific approach to creative thinking.

Basically a philosophy of life, the Huna system incorporates the knowledge of religion, psychology and psychic science. The religious aspect is the simplest, most complete system known. Huna concepts of sin, salvation, and the significance of life are completely free from the dogmas found in most of the world's faiths. The psychological aspects demonstrate the importance of self-suggestion and relaxation in creative thought techniques; while the constructs of Huna readily explain all facets of psychic phenomena.

W.R. Glover

CONTENTS

Chapter I

"The Code Language"

One of the oldest and best kept secrets in the world has been undergoing thorough, investigative and analytical research during this last century. It is a secret which combines psychology with religion, perhaps the finest and best system of this kind that the world has ever known; and yet, modern man nearly lost this fundamental knowledge.

Much of this psychology has been "rediscovered" and presented to us under the label of "POSITIVE THINKING." Numerous books have been written on the subject and most of us are familiar with the concepts offered by Norman Vincent Peale in his book "The Power of Positive Thinking."

"Think and Grow Rich" by Napoleon Hill, describes Andrew Carnegie's formula for personal achievement. Mr. Hill quotes such famous people as F. W. Woolworth, John Wanamaker, Woodrow Wilson and George Eastman, as all attributing their success to the principles of positive thought. Maxwell Maltz, in his well-read book "Psycho-Cybernetics," offers the reader self-improvement through programming suggestions into the subconscious mind and then utilizing the feedback mechanisms of cybernetics. However, most people who read these books try the techniques for awhile and then give up, because the psychology does not work for them.

Why do these positive thinking techniques often fail to produce the desired results? An ancient secret supplies the answer. The people who knew this secret system practiced a very sophisticated, but basic form, of positive thinking with spectacular results. Unfortunately, some of their more important concepts have not yet come into general knowledge. As a result, many people who have read books and have tried to "think positively" have found that the practice does not work for them.

At least seven thousand years ago, a group of people knew the principles of positive thinking; however, they understood the concepts far more clearly than do the schools of modern psychology. Their techniques were more sophisticated than those of today. With their additional knowledge, the ancient peoples who practiced this secret system performed what we now can only call miracles. Perhaps healings of the kind performed by Jesus Christ can be attributed to this secret system. Research leads to the conclusion that Christ was quite familiar with the concepts of this secret.

This secret contains much more than a successful method of creative thinking. It offers a philosophy of life that could be classified as a religion. The religious aspect seems to be the simplest, most complete and finest fundamental system so far developed. It stands on its own merits, and clarifies the basic tenets of many of the world's faiths.

Originally this system was without a name. It was handed down from parent to child through centuries and centuries. As this system was originally "rediscovered" in Hawaii, *Huna,* the Polynesian word for "secret" was selected. The "u" is pronounced like the double "oo" in moon. The Polynesian word for "priest" is *kahuna,* meaning "keeper of the secret."

The knowledge of *Huna* eventually spread by migration through several parts of the world. The initiatory material of this system was kept within a hereditary clan of priests. It was never written down. Instead, a special language was developed, which provided a means of giving both an inner and an outer meaning to any statement of the teachings. These dual meanings were similar to the initiatory statements of the lodges and brotherhoods that we have today. Only an initiate of the particular lodge can understand a particular secret phrase or statement. Similarly, only the *Huna* initiates could understand the inner meaning of a *Huna* phrase or statement.

Max Freedom Long spent the greater part of life researching this special language. He has written several books recording his findings which describe in detail the "code" as he calls it. He came upon the evidence that there had been such a system of knowledge almost by accident, and then devoted almost fifty years unearthing and correlating the bits and pieces, only recently coming in full possession of the priceless knowledge.

Many years ago Mr. Long became acquainted with Doctor William Tufts Brigham. At that time Dr. Brigham was the currator of the Bishop Museum of Natural History in Honolulu. At the time of his meeting with Mr. Long he had already spent forty years studying the Hawaiians, their society, religion and other aspects of their culture. Hearing that the Hawaiian priests, who were called *kahunas,* had firewalked on red hot lava as it flowed from a volcano, Mr. Long asked Dr. Brigham whether or not there was any truth in the reported fire-walking. "Yes," he said, "these *kahuna* priests fire-walked in my early days here in Hawaii." He went on to tell how he himself had walked across red hot lava. He had burned off his heavy mountain boots and socks, yet his feet remained unburned. No one had treated his feet. All that the natives did was to pray for protection from the heat, and this protection was given.

Continuing this questioning, Mr. Long learned that these kahuna priests had also done remarkable healings.

"What have these people got?" he demanded.

Dr. Brigham replied, "A system of psychology and religion, which is pure enough and close enough to its source, whatever that is, to work for them. I have tried for forty years to learn how they perform their magic, but to no avail. The secret lore is very sacred to the native priests."

After this meeting with Dr. Brigham, Mr. Long spent the next sixteen years in Hawaii trying to find the meaning behind the chants and prayers of the Hawaiian priests. He continued the research later in California and by 1936 had gained a fair knowledge of the basic principles of the secret lore.

Archaeologists have established that the present inhabitants of the Polynesian archipelago originally migrated from the Asian mainland. A study of Huna and its origins agrees with these findings. Werner Wolf, in his 1948 book "Island of Death," discusses the similarity of the Egyptian glyph writings and the "Paddle Board" writings of the natives of Easter Island in the Pacific. He suggests some ancient tie between the Egyptians and the Easter Island branch of the Polynesians. Mr. Long's research definitely suggests that the present day Polynesians have their origins in ancient Egypt.

His first book, "Recovering the Ancient Magic," was published in England. Among those who read it was Reginald Stewart, a war correspondent, who as a young man had learned of this same ancient lore from a tribe of Berbers in the Atlas mountains of North Africa.

An old woman, called a *"Quahine,"* had demonstrated the workability of the ancient system. In fact, she took young Stewart as a blood son and started to teach him, together with her seventeen-year-old daughter, the ancient beliefs and practices. Unfortunately, she had only made a beginning of her instructions when she was accidentally killed by a stray bullet from a battle going on in a valley between two waring tribes. As there was no other teacher to be found, Stewart returned to

England, carrying his notes with him. Years later when reading Mr. Long's book, he realized that Long was writing about the same system he had learned, in part, from her. Many of the special words that his teacher had used to describe her beliefs were almost identical to the Hawaiian. He sent Long a letter and soon was sharing what he knew. Together they managed to piece together the basics of the secret lore.

Among other things which the Quahine or "Woman Kahuna" had told Stewart was the legendary story of how her tribe had once been a part of twelve sub-tribes who had known and used Huna concepts, and who had lived in the Sahara Desert when it was still a green and fertile land of flowing rivers. As the rivers dried, the tribes foresaw that their lore was in danger of extinction. Concerned, they used their psychic powers to look about the world for a place to which they could move, an area where they would find safety for their beliefs. The place that they chose was the isolated Pacific.

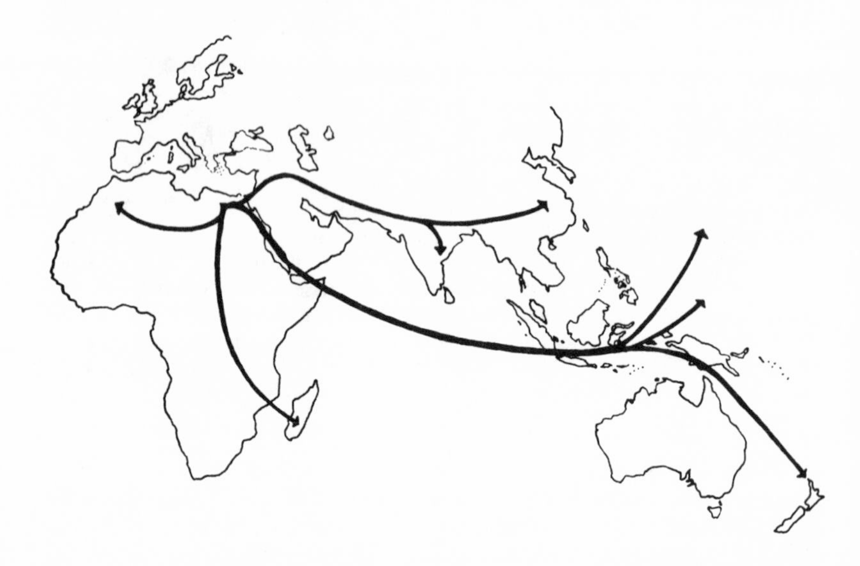

The tribes left Egypt and went in large double canoes down the Red Sea into the Indian Ocean, and eventually made their way to the far Pacific Isles. There were, she said, twelve tribes; however, her tribe remained behind as a rear guard lest the others be detained by the rulers of the period. They eventually reached the Atlas mountain area where they were able to preserve the secret lore. These tribes, she declared, were the original lost tribes of Israel.

The eleven tribes which got away divided. At least one tribe traveled along the coast of Africa to Madagascar. Some evidentally settled there, since half of the island today, over two thousand years later, is inhabited by a light brown people, who speak a language which is one of the Polynesian dialects, called Malagasy.

Other Huna people migrated through Arabia and into India. In India they left traces of their ideas, but little of their language. Whereas in Madagascar the **language** provides the evidence, in India it comes from the **ideas** which were left behind. The Kahunas must have made friends with the religious men of that period. Apparently, the teachers of Yoga were initiated into the Huna beliefs. Unfortunately, the beliefs gradually became contaminated. As an example, breathing exercises, vital to the practitioners of Huna, are also important in Yoga. However, the yogis began to experiment and over the years most of the Huna concepts became mixed and muddled, until finally very little of the practical application of the original system exists in Yoga today.

On the other hand, the original Huna beliefs were still pure when Buddha established his doctrine as a reform of the Brahmanism of his day. Obviously, there was a knowledge of Huna on the part of Buddha and his followers, because there are esoteric elements of Buddhism which can be understood only by knowing the Huna system. For example, the concept of attaining Nirvana, ordinarily understood as blending back into the source of all life and thus ceasing to exist, takes on an entirely different meaning when one understands Huna.

From India the ten remaining initiate tribes migrated through the Sumatra and Java straits. The Madagascar tribe did not join them. In the islands of the Pacific are ten different dialects of the Polynesian tongue represented in New Zealand, in Hawaii, in Tahiti, in Samoa and in the smaller islands of the Pacific area.

Because of the remote location of these islands, the people were able to preserve their beliefs and practice them for over two thousand years, free from the influence of other beliefs. The Huna people evidently settled in the Polynesian Islands before the writing of the Four Gospels because when the missionaries arrived in Hawaii, they were surprised to find that the natives knew all the main stories of the Old Testament, but knew nothing that was contained in the New Testament. Their legends told the story of the creation of Adam and Eve and the Garden. They had a close account of Noah and the Flood. They even knew of Jonah and the Whale. These were stories that had come from Chaldea and Babylonia, when the Jews were in captivity there. However, in none of the Hawaiian legends can be found even a trace of the story of Jesus or Mary or the Crucifixion. The missionaries, who arrived in Hawaii in

1820, could not understand how the natives had learned the Old Testament stories. If early explorers had taught stories of Adam and Eve, they certainly would have told of Jesus and his disciples.

Following the migration to Polynesia, the system flourished. The kahunas, who knew the secret system of positive thinking, were healers. They could heal broken bones, often in an instant. They were also able to look into the future. Then the missionaries arrived. The kahunas were impressed by their claim that Jesus performed healing miracles and, quite naturally, assumed that the Christians knew all about the Huna system. The missionary doctors, however, could not heal their sick as readily as the kahuna healers. So the natives eventually realized that these Christians, while they had the outer semblance of some Huna, did not know the complete working system.

As the missionaries obtained political influence over the chiefs, the kahunas were outlawed. The younger generation, the daughters and the sons who normally would have taken initiation and would have learned the secret, did not undertake the necessary training. Gradually, as the older kahunas began to die, the secret lore began to die as well. Huna, after having been kept pure and intact throughout all the centuries, became lost.

Mr. Long realized that the Hawaiian kahunas must have had special words in their language to use to teach their beliefs to the younger priests. He began to study any words in the Hawaiian dictionary, which might have to do with man's mental or spiritual nature. Immediately, he found unmistakable words which describe the "parts of mind," as they are called in modern psychology. After years of searching, he had started to learn the secret lore. Years passed before he found a "code" hidden in their language which told what they believed. This "code" aided him in discovering similar beliefs in other civilizations.

This code was built on a language which must have been identical phonetically to the language of the Huna tribes while they were in Egypt. In some of the lands visited by the migrating Huna tribes words of their language were left behind. Often these words became modified. Fortunately the kahunas in Hawaii preserved their language with great care, because within their language lay a "code" which described their secret system. If the language had been changed, key words would have been modified and the code would have never been preserved.

In order to keep their language pure, young kahunas were trained to memorize long chants covering the history of the people and the genealogy of the chiefs. If, while chanting these genealogies and legendary histories, a young priest changed a word, syllable, or a pronunciation, he was immediately corrected by the older kahunas. As a result, the language in Hawaii remained unchanged over thousands of years. Language modifications occurred in New Zealand, and to a greater degree, in Tahiti. But the Hawaiian language remained the purest and was the language Long used to find the key words to break the code and recover the ancient techniques of positive thinking.

The Hawaiian, like other Polynesian dialects, is a simple language. It is not agglutinated and does not change words to make tense or gender or number, instead it uses special words to show these changes. Hawaiian words are built from short root words, which together describe the full meaning of the idea. Since many root words have multiple meanings, it was ideal for a code language. Mr. Long found that by translating each root, he could find the hidden meaning, or code meaning, of the key words in the kahuna chants.

What complicated the breaking of the code is that certain words were used as the **symbol** of some part or element of the Huna system. If the symbolic meaning was not known, the true meaning of the statement could not be understood. For instance, in early Egypt the little pictured glyph of a grasshopper is to be found in the tombs with the mummy. In Hawaii the grasshopper was also a symbol for the same concept. The Hawaiian word for grasshopper is *unihipili.* The definition given in the Andrews "Hawaiian-English Dictionary" of 1865 is "one name of a class of gods, while *aumakua* is another. They were departed spirits of decomposed persons." Only by translating and considering the meaning of the roots of the words can one get at the real Huna meaning. It was the word used by the kahunas to indicate what we call the subconscious. None of the roots have anything to do with a grasshopper or with spirits or with a mummy of the deceased, but they all describe some characteristic of the subconscious mind.

The root *pili* means "united or joining" or "belonging to a person," and "to adhere to something." The subconscious is "joined to" and "belongs to" the body of the man. The root *nihi* describes "secretiveness, working silently and softly." The subconscious mind is certainly silent. The root *u* means a self, an "I." The priests had an alternate word, *uhinipili,* for the subconscious, which repeats some of the root words, but contains others which provide additional meanings. *Uhi* carries the meaning of "a weak voice, which is smothered by another voice." Another meaning is "to hide or be secretive." All these descriptions aptly describe the subconscious mind and the way it works. They show that it is secretive, that it is closely attached to the conscious mind, that it will do things only when it wishes to do so, and that it also hides things, such as complexes, and is the center of the emotions.

Uhane is Hawaiian for the conscious mind. *U* means a "self" and *hane* means "to talk." The root words gave the description of the conscious mind, the self which talks. The human being is the only animal which is able to talk to convey ideas.

These examples show the method used in finding the hidden meanings in words used by the kahunas. The code was really quite simple. The separate meanings of the root words describe the idea that is hidden in the word.

The Hawaiian code word for the Superconscious is *Aumakua*. *Makua* means "parental" or "a pair of gods," and it is the "parental" part of man. The roots also mean "very old." The translation for the word *aumakua* given by a student of Hawaiian lore is "utterly trustworthy parental spirit." The Hawaiian dictionary translates the word as "one who can be trusted as a child trusts a parent." One could call the superconscious: "God who is trusted to love the subconscious and conscious with whom it is connected." It will help us and guide us throughout our life.

The kahunas did not conceal their secret teachings only in coded words. They also used symbols. These were more difficult to understand because they simply used various words as symbols of something. For instance, "water" was the symbol of the life force of the human being. They used the word "seed" in lieu of "prayer." The word "path" denoted the connection between the conscious and subconscious parts of man to the Superconscious. "Light" was the symbol for the Superconscious.

Anyone who wishes to check on these Huna code words can purchase a good Hawaiian-English dictionary to use in examining the clever way in which the early kahunas placed double meanings in words and roots of compound words to conceal the inner meanings while being able to make sense with the outer meaning. The language is very simple to work with and with the additional knowledge of a few key symbol words, one can easily run a check on the Huna findings.

By the end of the Second World War, Mr. Long had gradually developed a full understanding of this code and the symbols; however, it took nearly forty years for him to become well versed. It was not until 1965 that he was able to tabulate the complete, workable psychology of the ancient system of positive thinking called Huna.

By then he had researched and found references to this code in religions such as early Yoga, the later Hinduism, as well as Buddhism. The Greeks and Egyptians had elaborate mystery plays which were used for teaching and in the initiation of younger members. Mr. Long discovered specific key phrases of the Huna system coded into these sacred writings of the mystery cults of the Middle East.

Very little of the Vedic material of India was found to correspond with Huna; however, in the later "Upanishads," statements appear which resemble Huna beliefs and practices. More coded statements were found in the "Egyptian Book of the Dead" and in the famous Hindu epic, the "Bhagavad Gita." He even found traces of the ancient system coded into Genesis, Isaiah and Jeremiah. Surprisingly, the Four Gospels of our New Testament contain more coded Huna than any other religious writing.

Chapter II

"The Three Selves of Man"

Every religion has a version of the creation of man. The early initiates of the lore of Huna often told tales which explained concepts of their secret science. One of these legends tells that when the gods created man they used two kinds of clay, red and white. In this way man was able to have two spirits live in him. In modern terms, the man of two colors of clay contains a conscious and a subconscious pair of minds, or spirits, or "selves."

The ancient kahunas regarded the conscious and the subconscious minds of man as two separate and distinct entities. They considered the conscious mind as simply the "self" that could talk, which lived as a guest within the animal body. It could observe facts and then rationalize these facts logically. The major job of the conscious mind was to guide and direct the subconscious mind or self.

The modern school of psychology **recognizes** the subconscious; however, the kahunas **understood** it. They knew its abilities and how to put it to work. To them the subconscious was regarded as an animal self. This animal self had, like all animals, instinctive guidance to direct it to grow, breathe, digest food, and perform all the involuntary functions. Today we know that the subconscious controls our automatic responses such as auto reflexes. All animals are controlled by their emotions, and the subconscious is the center of our emotional being. The conscious mind's job is to rationalize and control our emotions. The kahunas regarded the subconscious self as a storehouse for the thoughts and impressions of the conscious self. Today we often liken it to a computer in that it serves as a memory bank, but lacks the power to reason logically. The subconscious mind must rely on the conscious mind for inductive reasoning. The conscious mind can "act as a guide," as the ancients put it, and control the subconscious mind through suggestion.

While the subconscious was said to have one's memories as its chief possession, the conscious self possessed the power of speech. It was believed that only when the conscious self was able to act as a guest in the bodily house did the human animal talk. The Egyptians made a god of the power of speech. It was "The Word," and in Christianity we meet the idea in a very similar form: "In the beginning was the Word, and the Word was God."

Also living as a part of the human consciousness is the Superconscious. This term was used by psychologists such as Jung and others; Freud called it the "Super Ego"; more recent schools of psychology have termed it the "Universal Mind" or "Universal Conscious." It may be compared to the "Guardian Angel" of some religions. The kahunas believed it had evolved much farther than the two lower selves and acted as a sort of personal god who, at one time, was a member of one's clan or family. This self did not live in the body and could travel to far places. It was, nevertheless, considered as a distinct part of the man.

The Egyptian kahuna priests spoke of these three selves, or minds, as the "I" or middle self, "The Son" or lower animal self, and "The Holy Spirit" or High Self. Christians say: "Father, Son and Holy Ghost." For convenience sake, we refer to these three minds as the "low self," the "middle self," and the "High Self."

To the kahunas the High Self was not absolute God. They believed that there were many levels of Higher Selves and, if necessary, one's High Self could obtain assistance from the *Akua-aumakuas,* who stand one grade higher than the High Self. They did not concern themselves with ultimate God, because they knew that man could obtain all that he could require by simply having an understanding of and a working relationship with his own third level of mind, his High Self.

The term "low self" does not mean that the subconscious is low in a degraded sense. It simply means that it is the lowest of the three selves on a scale of growth or evolution.

The kahunas evidently considered the low self something that must be thoroughly understood. Their root meanings for the word, *unihipili,* accurately describes its characteristics.

First, it is a separate and conscious entity, just as are the middle self and the High Self. It is the servant of the other selves and is attached to the middle self as a younger brother. It cleaves to it as if they were two parts of a thing which had been glued together. The low self has control of all the various processes of the physical body, except the voluntary muscles. It is the animal part of the human being. It, and it alone, is the seat of the emotions. It is the one who sheds tears. If one disbelieves this, let him try to shed tears of grief all by himself as a conscious middle self and see how impossible it is. Tears will not flow until the emotion of grief has been aroused in the subconscious. On the other hand, one may unexpectedly read, see, or hear something which touches the emotions and the low self reacts of its own accord and embarrasses us by a sudden shedding of tears.

Love, hate, and fear all come from the low self as emotions, and they may be so strong that they sweep away the "will" of the middle self and force it to join in the feeling of the emotion. The understanding of this is important, because we are often carried away by the emotions of the low self, and in this way are over-powered by it. The major job of the middle self is to learn to control the low self, and prevent it from running our lives.

The low self is the one which can be influenced or controlled by hypnotic suggestion. It may hold unrationalized ideas, ideas which the middle self was not in a condition to rationalize when they were formed. If it reacts to these unrationalized ideas, we develop what is known as a "complex."

The low self also performs the function of recording every impression and every thought. All sounds, sights, thoughts, or words come in units, which contain many single impressions joined together. The kahunas symbolized these as clusters of small round things, such as grapes or seeds. Our subconscious responds swiftly to the commands of our conscious mind in recalling these memories so that the impression given when we talk or write is that we of the conscious middle self have all the memories right in the hand for immediate use.

As has been explained, the low self is purely animal with the lesser, deductive power of reason. It is the seat of the emotions and of the memory. Remembering memories of former experience, the low self arrives at a conclusion. Its will or desire is always based on memories of former expectancies. The middle self of man, however, cannot remember. It has no emotions. It uses an inductive power of reason. The High Self of man has a superior power of reason that is beyond the understanding of most men. For a normal human being to understand the reasoning power of the High Self would be akin to a normal five-year-old understanding calculus.

One of the most important techniques in the Huna concepts is understanding the lines of communication between the three minds or "selves," as the kahunas called them. A unique concept in the Huna technique of prayer is that the subconscious and not the conscious mind has the telephone line to the High Self. So, if we wish to pray to the High Self (or God), to make our request, we have to go **through** the subconscious. It is not possible to pray directly to the High Self. The most important part of the mechanism of **this** kind of positive thinking is learning to work through the subconscious to get to the Super-conscious.

Try to think of the three selves of man as a house with a basement, a first floor, and an attic. The middle self lives on the first floor; it can see out the windows to get a glimpse of the world. There are trees and shrubs to block the view, however, and so the information gathered by the middle self may not be correct.

The low self lives in the basement. There are no windows. The only "facts" given to the low self are pictures sent through a telepathic telephone line from the middle self on the first floor. The subconscious does not question these "facts," it simply accepts them as presented and files them away as "memory."

Now the Superconscious lives in the attic. This High Self can see all around through its windows. No shrubbery blocks the view. It sees pure truth. However, and this is extremely important, the High Self's telephone line goes only to the low self in the basement. It cannot communicate directly to the middle self or conscious mind. This is the reason why we must pray through the subconscious in order to reach the High Self. **There is no direct telephone line from the conscious to the Superconscious!!!**

This ancient concept seems to have originated, or at least first appeared, in the religious beliefs of the ancient Assyrian and Babylonian countries in Chaldea and in Egypt. The Egyptians preserved much information about this belief in their hieroglyphics, or picture writing. As an example, the stork is an ancient symbol of a spirit or supernatural being. In the picture writing found in the early Egyptian temples and tombs are many glyphs showing three storks collapsed together to become almost one, standing for the three united selves of the man.

Chapter III

"Mana, the Life Force"

We must keep in mind that the ancients used what we call "constructs" to describe their beliefs. A construct is a method of analyzing something **as if** it were the case. It really does not matter whether the actual construct is accurate, so long as the end result is accurate. Constructs are used today to describe phenomena we really do not fully understand, such as electrical energy and light energy.

The Huna construct of man maintains that he is comprised of three selves, or minds, and a physical body. These three selves are designated as the middle self, or conscious mind; the low self, or subconscious mind; and the High Self, or Superconscious mind. Each of these selves utilizes its own energy or life force to function.

The Hawaiian kahuna called this energy *mana.* Mana is a construct for a force, which, if properly used, can do work in the form of obtaining desired results through creative thinking. This force, this extra something, which might be compared to the vitamins in food, cannot be seen or measured by scientific instruments; however, it has been integral to many ancient religions and beliefs, and has not been accepted by modern psychology. According to the Huna concepts, the low self makes this vital life force from the food, air, and water which we consume. It utilizes this force to function as a "mind" or "self."

The Polynesian word for this life force is *mana.* We encounter this word in the Old Testament, but with two *n*'s. The mystery of the "manna" in the story becomes no mystery at all, when it is understood that it was the mana of the "life force" which fell from heaven to rejuvenate the Israelites in the desert.

The early men of India used the word *prana* for this life force. They believed that more than one kind of this energy existed, and over the centuries they developed a system of prana forces for every action of man.

One can easily compare mana energy with electricity. This is a pertinent comparison, since mana involves other concepts similar to those of electricity. Electricity can be generated, held in storage (as in a battery) and then discharged to perform work. The mana manufactured by the low self is like a static electrical charge, in that it can be accumulated and stored in the body until needed. It also has positive and negative poles. The Chinese express this energy polarity in their Yin-Yang concept.

A similar case is the Easter Island concept of mana. Their symbol for the polar energies of life were the navel, for energy leading outward, and the uterus, for energy turned inward. This same concept also existed in the Mayan civilization.

Mana is not, however, like ordinary electricity which meets variations in resistance as it flows through different substances. Mana seems to pass through **any** substance with no decrease in energy level. It does not weaken with increase in distance of transmission as we find in radio waves. Telepathic messages, which are sent with the use of this energy, have been known to travel to the other side of the earth without weakening. This energy may be a difficult concept for some to accept. However, just fifty years ago the concept of television was hard to believe. Evidence that the human body generates power sufficient to transmit thoughts over thousands of miles was reported in a symposium of Russian and American scientists in 1968. Dr. I. Kogan of the Popov Institute said that conclusions based on 1966-1967 experiments indicate that thoughts may be conveyed by extremely long electromagnetic waves with crests ranging from 16 to 600 miles apart. Kogan reported that calculations indicate the human body generates four to five times the energy needed for long distance telepathy; energy sufficient to "keep in touch with astronauts in case electronic communications break down." Dr. R. Moss, assistant professor of medical psychology at U.C.L.A., told the symposium of findings "very similar to Dr. Kogan's."

The Australian, Youlden-Johnson, experimented with this energy by causing a thermometer to rise 11½ degrees above room temperature simply by pointing his finger toward the mercury bulb. Madam David-Neil, in her books, tells of seeing men in Tibet sitting beside a frozen lake wrapped in a wet sheet. They had to control their vital energy to create heat sufficient to dry the sheet in order to pass initiation into certain orders. Conversely, certain cults in India use their *prana* forces to keep from being burned, while fire walking as a test of their inner growth.

Much testing and experimental work must be done before modern man will know as much about mana energy as the old kahuna initiates knew. One element of their psychology, which modern psychology has yet to consider, is that life force is an energy that can be transferred from oneself to another. For instance, in Hawaii the kahunas helped in battle by charging sticks with low mana and then throwing them over the heads of their warriors. When a stick touched one of the enemy, the mana discharged like a large charge of static electricity and knocked the enemy cold. Women trained for the task also stood behind the battle lines. When a warrior was fatigued he fell out of the ranks: one of the women recharged him with mana so that he could go back into the fray. Mr. Stewart's experiences with the African Berbers offers additional understanding of the nature of this energy. Among other demonstrations made by the Quahine was her mental direction of a large accumulated charge of this force; she directed it to push the heavy door of a storage cave through its frame and into the cave's interior.

Mesmerism is a similar use of the mana charge. Two hundred years ago Dr. Anton Mesmer became famous throughout Europe by using a force he called "Animal Magnetism" to obtain spectacular healings. He believed this force would flow from his body into his patient to produce a healing. He often caused so much vital force to flow that his patient was rendered unconscious. This condition became known as "mesmeric shock." In 1950 a mesmerist in Los Angeles used to demonstrate his power by charging himself and then pointing his finger at one after another of volunteer subjects seated in a row. Each one, when pointed at, would slump and slide to the floor unconscious. The heavy charge of mana caused the low self to lose consciousness for a short time.

The kahunas of old believed there were three grades of mana. In more modern terms, one might call them different levels of life energy. Low mana is obtained by the low self to enable our physical bodies to function as living animals. Some of this energy is shared with the middle self and the High Self. This basic energy, when used as the life force of the middle self, is changed in some subtle way. The kahunas thought of it as a dividing of the basic mana and called it *mana-mana,* indicating by doubling the word that this higher level of energy had more power, and that it could be used by the middle self to command and control the low self. This force is termed as "will" or "will power" by modern psychology. The High Self also needs mana to operate on its plane of existence. This highest energy level was called *mana loa,* meaning "the strongest," by the Hawaiians. Thus the three levels of energy are *mana,* used by the low self, *mana-mana,* used by the middle self, and *mana loa,* used by the High Self.

The introductory chapter covered the secret code language used by the keepers of the secret of Huna to prevent outsiders from learning their powerful magic. The kahunas also used symbols to stand for key words. Finding the Polynesian word *wai,* meaning "water," was used consistently in compound words or phrases where mana was under discussion, Mr. Long learned that "water" was their symbol for mana. Water, "overflowing as from a fountain," was the symbol of a heavy charge of vital force.

One can think of the three "selves" as energy levels. With the advent of the quantum theory, our understanding of the world in which we live has undergone a tremendous transformation. Instead of a world of dead, inert matter, we are now confronted with a world of motion in the form of energy. What we call matter is seen to be the structural arrangement of energy fields, ranging from the simple hydrogen molecule to the most complex protein molecules. We ourselves are living fields of energy levels.

Scientists talk of man as a field of energy; Huna simply says there are three basic levels of this energy, each with its own potential. While the low self or subconscious uses energy as the life force of the body, the middle self or conscious mind uses its grade or energy potential as "will" or hypnotic force. The High Self takes the energy as a gift from the lower selves and changes it in some subtle way. This change in the potential, once it is taken by the High Self, is not completely understood. It has been likened to a change in voltage or vibration rate. As the High Self can use its energy to produce answers to our prayers, this change or energy difference lies in the **use** of the energy by the particular self or mind.

Of the three selves, only the low self of the physical body is capable of creating life force from the food and water and air which we consume. The middle self takes some of this life force and changes its voltage, or its rate of vibration, to become a hypnotic force. It can be used by the conscious mind to give self-suggestion to one's low self, or it can be used by a hypnotic operator to give suggestion to another low self. This is the mechanism of hypnosis. The suggestion is passed by word of mouth, or it can be accomplished silently through thought. In order to obtain answers to our prayers, and to make changes in our circumstances, the High Self needs a large supply of vital force. One of the basic things that we learn in Huna is how to accumulate an extra amount of vital force, and then how to send it to the High Self. The future, which has been built in conformity with the hopes and fears, and acts of the lesser two minds or selves of the body, may be changed by the High Self through positive thinking techniques to break down the patterns in existence and to build new and better patterns to replace them.

The kahunas believed that by an action of mind a man can create additional energy to accumulate a surcharge of mana when needed. They felt that hard breathing would assist in creating this vital force. This theory is supported by our medical doctors, who have found that our food is digested and then changed to glycogen, or blood sugar. This is then oxidized with the oxygen we breathe and gives us our strength to live. Since the low self controls all our bodily functions, it can burn more blood sugar by taking in more air to create mana.

A very ancient Yoga exercise to increase vital energy, "prana," is to sit under a tree in a secluded place, cross-legged, with the hands resting on the knees. Then inhale, absorbing prana from the earth; exhale, transferring to oneself. Another exercise is to sit cross-legged with arms held above the head; concentrate on drawing prana from the ether, through the fingertips. Another is to expose the body to the sun; inhale, absorbing its energy; exhale, transferring it to oneself. The late Dr. Oscar Brunler, stood on tiptoes and raked the air with his fingers, first reaching up as high as he could and then swinging his arms in a circle while he bent his body to allow his hands to reach the ankles. He believed that this force was alive in the air. Baron Fersen toured the United States some years ago giving lectures on what he called the "Universal Life Force," which he felt could be drawn out of the air and stored in his body. He would stand with feet spread and arms extended and pick up the charge as a radio antenna picks up radio waves. He would then affirm, "The Universal Life Force is flowing through me . . . I can feel it."

All these techniques have two things in common. First, a strong mental effort is made to imagine oneself becoming charged with energy; and second, breathing exercises are performed, or some physical activity which automatically results in heavy breathing. When the kahunas wished to accumulate a surcharge of mana, they breathed deeply and visualized mana rising like water rises in a fountain, higher and higher, until it overflows. The subconscious knows how to accumulate vital energy. That is its job; it does so every time you stand up or sit down. Breathing is automatic to the low self, and when you consciously begin to breathe, slowly and deeply, the low self is impressed. It pays close attention to the thoughts and desires of the conscious mind. Once you have its attention, you simply explain what is wanted and then ask the low self to do it.

It is best to relax before starting to accumulate extra mana. Sit or lie still for a while and try to still the mind. This is most important, because you must have the cooperation of the low self in order to obtain a surcharge of energy. The low self will not pay attention to your desires if your mind is thinking about a business or household problem. Tell your low self that you want to accumulate a charge of mana and you want its cooperation. Talk to it as you would talk to a child. Then say to yourself, which is really saying to your low self, "Now we will start accumulating extra vital force. This accumulation will go on steadily while I breathe more heavily. This will burn more blood sugar and will create mana energy."

While breathing, you must **imagine** that you are accumulating the energy. Some people think of filling a jar with water, some visualize water being stored as in a dam, others "feel" a flow of energy surging through their body. One technique is to imagine a small ball of light, which grows brighter and larger each time a breath is taken. The important thing is to imagine yourself accumulating this extra energy. You must bring yourself to believe that your low self is actually generating and storing this mana within your body.

The breathing technique is done in a rhythmic cadence. The kahunas called it the *Ha,* or "Breath Rite.' This word *Ha* means "to breathe more heavily" or "to breathe strongly." It also means "slow, deep breaths." Breathe in and out until you complete four cycles. *Ha* also has a root meaning of "four." Then, in order to avoid getting too much oxygen and becoming dizzy, pause for a while. Many people find they soon fall into a kind of evenness or rhythm in counting the breaths by fours. The slowness or deepness of the breathing has no definite limits, and one must try to learn from practice what seems most natural.

The "heartbeat count" rhythm is often used. While holding the commanding thought that the low self is beginning to accumulate mana, you begin to breathe just a little more strongly. Keep in step with the heartbeat. Breathe in: one, two, three, four. When four inhalations and exhalations have been completed, pause for a few heartbeats. Then the next four breaths can be taken. If you begin to feel light-headed or have some unwanted sensation, the pause between sets of four breaths can be lengthened. Continue this count until forty sets of breaths have been taken. Ten sets is often sufficient.

It takes a little practice to develop the heartbeat rhythm into a standard technique of accumulation. At first the attention will be fastened on the "count" and the expectation of an accumulation of mana may be neglected. But with practice, the rhythm can become habitual and one can concentrate on the accumulation.

There is no particular physical sensation after obtaining an extra charge of mana. Some people feel a tingling in their hands. The individual with a low normal level of mana can usually sense this addition of energy. It adds to his sense of well-being, sharpens the mind, and makes the senses more acute. It is surprising how much clearer the vision becomes and how much more detail and color one can see after taking on a surcharge of mana.

Perhaps the "Ha Rite" of deep breathing can be explained by the Operon Theory developed by Drs. Jacob and Monad, who received the Nobel Prize in 1965 for their work. Their premise was to explain how environmental changes can effect cell metabolism. Metabolism without oxygen will produce two units of energy; however, in the presence of oxygen, 38 units are produced.

Many of you may have a knowledge of the Yoga breathing practices where special postures and positions are specified. The Huna technique requires no particular positions in order to acquire mana. You may sit, stand, lie down, walk, or be driving your car. The posturings of the Yogi are simply a technique to impress his low self, to get its attention. You may feel that a special position helps, or you may like to burn incense, or ring a bell. Anything that will help jar your low self and make it pay attention to your desire is helpful. Use any technique that you like, but do not feel this is mandatory for generating life force.

The important thing is to relax and get the attention and cooperation of your low self. Then you must visualize the accumulation of the energy. Store it in your body, or in a visualized glass, or whatever suits you. There is no set rule.

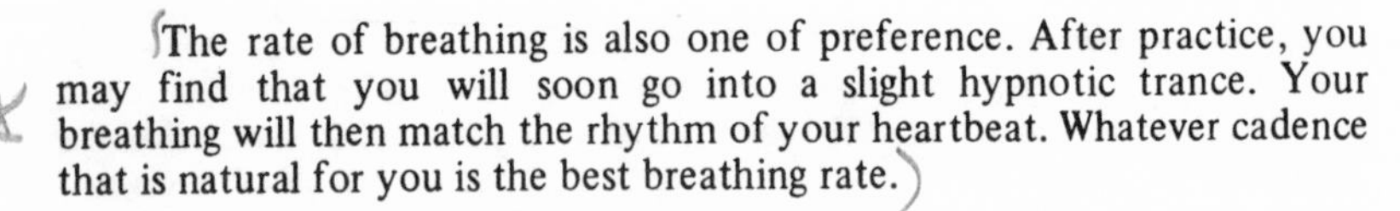

The rate of breathing is also one of preference. After practice, you may find that you will soon go into a slight hypnotic trance. Your breathing will then match the rhythm of your heartbeat. Whatever cadence that is natural for you is the best breathing rate.

It is important to remember that creating mana is a very natural action of the low self. The most important part of the Huna technique is to sincerely believe that your low self has generated an extra supply of mana.

There is an interesting story connected to the "Ha Rite" and the importance of deep breathing when accumulating mana for use in the Huna prayer technique.

When the missionaries first arrived in Hawaii, they told the kahunas of the healing miracles of Jesus. The kahunas thought these missionaries knew all about the Huna religion and assumed that they were great healers.

The Hawaiians were used to a slow, careful preparation for prayer. The kahunas often spent two or three hours to consider and contemplate their prayer. Then the vital force was accumulated by the deep breathing of the people seated outside the stone temple. Finally the prayer was put into words and sent to the great company of High Selves, the High Selves of all the people, asking for and picturing blessings for their tribe. However, when the Polynesians saw the missionaries stand and without any preparation begin to pray and then say "amen" without any pause or sending of vital force, the natives shook their heads and said, "These people make a prayer that is not strong. These people are without breath." In the Hawaiian language the word *Ha* is "breath," and the word for "without" is *Oli.* So they called the missionaries *ha-olis. Holis* is the word today, after shortening it. Since that time, all white people, all the people who pray without sending the vital force to the High Self, are all called *holis,* "the breathless ones," by the Hawaiians.

This story suggests one use that can be made of a large surcharge of mana energy is that of prayer. The middle self takes the base mana and changes it to mesmeric or hypnotic force. This energy level can then be used to strengthen self suggestions made by the middle self to the low self. The High Self also uses our mana in order to answer our prayer. Through prayer techniques, one can perform miracles which range all the way from simple healings to spectacular changes in physical conditions and even to changing the fabric of the future.

Chapter IV

"Self-Suggestion"

The African witch doctor does not know the meaning of psychology; yet he has mastered this art for centuries. It is an established fact that native believers of Voodoo can actually die from the power of suggestion. Suggestion can, of course, be used for positive purposes, and self-suggestion can aid us in many ways.

The power of suggestion has been known to modern man for only a short time, relatively speaking. As early as 1894, Dr. J. M. Fathergill wrote a book, entitled "The Will Power," which showed a knowledge of the subconscious. Two hundred years ago a French experimenter, Dr. Franz Anton Mesmer, inadvertently discovered that by using verbal suggestion and a strange power obtained through strong imagination he could produce healings in his patients. The English doctor, James Braid, used suggestion to cause another's low self to react to his command. We now call this form of self-suggestion "hypnosis."

Later, a New England professor, Dr. F. Pierce, discovered that physical relaxation was necessary for suggestion to be effective. The subconscious mind must be quieted and relaxed before it can be conditioned.

In the 1950's, when Duke University became the center for ESP studies under Dr. J. Rhine, a Dr. H. Hart came to Duke and experimented with autoconditioning. He believed one's "real" self suggests one's moods to his subconscious mind. He found his students could change their moods and general outlook through what he termed "autoconditioning." The success of his experiments was so marked that there could be no question of the validity of the results or of the outstanding benefits gained. It was found that nearly all the students could learn to autocondition quickly and with little trouble.

Since these pioneers, there have been many books presenting many facts on the power and the value of self-suggestion. The ancient psychology of Huna takes these facts and explains the **how** and the **why** of self-suggestion. To understand the rather intangible things involved in the use of suggestion, let us consider the phenomenon of hypnosis.

Hypnosis is a very powerful use of the power of suggestion. A hypnotist puts his subject to sleep in order to get the middle self completely relaxed and out of the way. It is the low self that accepts suggestion; the reasoning middle self stands between the low self and the external suggestion. Once the middle self is in deep sleep, it cannot screen the suggestions, and the thoughts of the hypnotist will penetrate to the low self of the subject. When the suggestion is reinforced by a charge of vital force, the suggestion becomes firmly fixed within the subconscious of the subject.

The subject who has complete control over his low self can resist hypnotic suggestion. His middle self simply rationalizes everything and negates the suggestions. When the hypnotist suggests sleep, the subject simply says to himself, "No, I'm not going to sleep." Since the low self always obeys the thoughts of its master, the middle self, the hypnotist's suggestion of sleep is neutralized. If, however, the subject is perfectly relaxed, the middle self is unable to rationalize the suggestion and he soon falls into a trance-like sleep.

This example serves to demonstrate the importance of relaxation when using self-suggestion. Both the conscious and the subconscious minds must be relaxed. If the middle self mind is not quiet, it is difficult to concentrate on the desired thought. Peripheral thoughts will enter the mind and concentration will become difficult. A properly organized suggestion requires hard concentration on the part of the conscious mind, and all outside influences must be excluded.

As an experiment, try to quiet your mind and think of absolutely nothing for just sixty seconds. You will find it extremely difficult. Thoughts of the day's problems or desires will filter into your mind.

The subconscious mind must also be relaxed. The Huna theory offers an explanation of why the low self accepts suggestion more readily when we are physically relaxed. Huna tells us that administering suggestion is a process of the middle self planting a powerfully charged thought in the mind of the low self. When the low self and its animal body are both active, there is always a heavy charge of mana energy in the physical body. If the low self is as heavily charged as the middle self, it tends to reject the offered idea of the suggestion. But, if it is relaxed, requiring little energy, it becomes receptive and seems to attract the suggestion to itself.

This process can be likened to two batteries with their terminals connected. The battery with the higher potential or stronger charge will release some of its energy to fill the other; however, if both batteries are at the same potential, there will be no interchange of energy.

When the low self with its physical body is relaxed, it needs only a small amount of life force to function. The middle self can then draw much of the stored energy to its center of consciousness to pour a charge of "will" force into the suggestion and strengthen the suggestion.

The kahunas must have known the importance of relaxation, because their word for "to relax" was *hoolulu,* which also means "to sow or plant seeds," a symbol of planting tiny thought forms of suggested ideas in the consciousness of the low self. Their construct was really very simple. They believed a thought form was a real and concrete thing. To them, an idea was made of an invisible substance that was capable of absorbing mana or life force. They believed that a thought form is an impression molded into the body of the low self. This can be likened to an impression on a phonograph record. A number of related impressions make up a cluster of thought forms and such clusters contain the memories of complete events.

These thought forms are capable of absorbing life energy. Mana strengthens the thought or memory. As an example, add the emotional energy of hate to some bad memory and it will become so strong as to become an obsession. Similarly, dwell on some positive thought, reinforce it with the emotional energy of desire, and you can strengthen this thought form to a condition of reality.

The Huna symbol for a thought form was a "seed." One could not see the plant inside the seed, it was invisible. Yet, to the native mind of the kahunas, the full grown plant was actually inside the seed. One planted the seed, nourished it, and the result was a plant. Similarly, one planted a seed of thought in one's subconscious mind, nourished this thought with life force, and the result was the desired thought.

The Hawaiian word for seed is *ano-ano.* The root has the meaning of "to change the state of things" or "changing present conditions to become new."

There is an interesting story in relation to this concept of a thought form as a seed. In the Seventh Century, Nestorian missionaries traveled into China and taught a version of Christian ethics, which also contain

Huna concepts. By far the most open presentation of the Huna system is found in an ancient Chinese book, "The Secret of the Golden Flower," which is available in translation. The story tells of planting a seed in God's Garden, which grows toward the light when it is watered daily. The *seed* is the suggestion. The seed grows toward *light,* which is the Huna symbol of the High Self. The seed requires *water,* which is the Huna symbol for mana or the life force.

The importance of strengthening a thought form with a charge of vital force cannot be over emphasized.

Dr. Franz Anton Mesmer became famous throughout Europe by using a force he called "Animal Magnetism" to obtain spectacular healings. Dr. Mesmer believed he could draw this magnetic force from magnets held in his hands and, once charged, cause this force to enter and heal his patient.

To explain this phenomenon by using the Huna constructs, Dr. Mesmer imagined or visualized himself accumulating a large charge of magnetism and inadvertently caused his low self to create a very large charge of mana. When he touched his patient to transfer the force, he administered a certain amount of telepathic suggestion. The **idea** of being healed was planted in the low self of his patient and, being highly charged with mana, the will of Dr. Mesmer's middle self so impressed the patient's low self as to cause it to react in the form of an instant healing.

Mesmer became very adept in accumulating mana and projecting it. He taught his method to others and by 1784 became the center of a storm of controversy within medical circles. Benjamin Franklin, who was the United States ambassador to France at the time, was a member of a committee which investigated Dr. Mesmer's claims and techniques. Eventually Mesmer conceded that holding a magnet in one's hands did not give one magical power; however, it could not be denied that some animal type of force was generated within the body and could be projected. Franklin was impressed and thereafter became very much interested in magnetism in general. We all know of his experiments of flying a kite in a rainstorm and obtaining indications of electricity from a key.

Suggestion, of the mesmeric or hypnotic type, is composed of an idea or thought form which has been strengthened by a charge of vital force and directed by the will of the middle self. This charged idea is introduced to the low self center of consciousness, where it then has the power to cause an appropriate reaction.

In France in the last generation, Dr. Coué taught people to **think** of themselves as healed. He administered suggestions to his patients by talking to their low selves, assuring them that their bodies would be getting well. He had his patients repeat day after day the phrase: "Every day, in every way, I am getting better and better." At one time, this formula was the rage throughout the Western world; however, it failed in its promise and people stopped using it. What was wrong? The answer is simple. The middle self was reciting words and the low self may have listened, but the middle self did not make the proper mental picture of the better or healed condition and then impress it suggestively on the relaxed low self.

Here is the key to positive thought: Faith! Belief! If you, the middle self, are not fully convinced that you are getting better each day, then the low self will not believe it either. If the low self does not believe it, it will not start making the body match the picture of the healed state. Mana goes where it is directed only if one has full confidence that the low self will generate and send this energy to strengthen the thought form. One's low self must believe that what is being suggested is possible and that results can be obtained.

Jesus taught: "According to your faith, so shall it be unto you." This statement is pure Huna. When we break a leg, we expect it to knit and the low self acts accordingly. But if we do not fully and completely believe that our backache can be healed, the low self will simply not respond to our positive suggestion and the ache will continue.

The goal of self-suggestion is to gain sufficient control of your low self to obtain its full cooperation in all the things that you, as a middle self, desire. With the cooperation of your low self, you can break habits you have had for years. Your low self can help in bettering health, reducing pain, providing peace of mind, or acquiring material riches.

Chapter V

"Relaxation and Suggestion Techniques"

Example Text

The Hawaiian kahunas had a phrase meaning "relax the mind," which translates: "relax the intestines." When we try to relax the mind, we must first relax the body. If we consciously quiet our mind, the low self will try to oblige; however, it will still tend to fidget and to let its thoughts wander.

Try an experiment. Sit in a comfortable position, lay your head back, and try to make your mind blank for sixty seconds. Try to still your mind so that no thoughts at all enter your consciousness. Do this for one full minute.

Most people will find this to be very difficult. Even though your middle self willed your low self to be quiet, your subconscious mind simply was not sufficiently relaxed to become completely stilled, extraneous thoughts filtered through.

Sit back again and tense all your muscles throughout your body. Hold this for a bit and then let go. Now, mentally command your low self to relax. Tell yourself, "I am going to relax every muscle in my body. I see myself as a large cat stretching my legs, my neck, my back. I see this cat stretch out and then flop back on the chair."

Now, say to yourself, "My toes are relaxed, my feet are completely limp, my ankles are relaxed. My legs feel like concrete and have no strength. My stomach muscles are now relaxed. My heart and my lungs are completely relaxed. My hands and fingers are very heavy. My arms are like heavy concrete. My shoulders and neck muscles are totally at rest. My neck has no strength at all. All the tension is drained away. My back is now completely relaxed . . . loose . . . the right side . . . the left side . . . the small of my back. All the tension flows away. I see myself as a great, limp cat . . . in a state of total rest and relaxation. All sounds that I hear are relaxing sounds.

I now command my subconscious mind, my low self, to put away all thoughts. I do not want a single idea or thought to enter my mind. I am going to remain like this for a full minute. During this time my entire body will remain at rest and my mind will remain stilled and empty of all thoughts."

After a pause of sixty seconds, tell yourself, "I am now going to generate mana from my breathing. I am gathering mana as I draw in more and more oxygen. My low self is creating this force and is storing it in my body. I am being made vital and strong and alive by this mana."

Now breathe in, long and slow, to the count of four heartbeats. Pause, and breathe out slowly, taking four heartbeats to completely exhale your breath. Hold a beat, and inhale, hold, and exhale. Continue this for a minute or two.

While breathing tell yourself, "I see Energy being created. I see it as water in a bowl. The bowl is getting full of water. I can see the water rising. After each breath I see more water in the bowl."

Continue breathing for another minute or so. Then say to yourself, "My vitality is building up, it grows stronger and stronger. Mana is flowing as water into the bowl. The water rises higher and higher in the bowl until it overflows. I now ask my low self to create one final amount of mana energy."

After another set of breaths, say with conviction, confidence **and emotion**: "My vitality has been made strong and I am filled with the desire to accomplish those things which I will now visualize. I can feel mana energy surging through my body. I now command my low self to store this energy, while I create thought forms. I wish to strengthen these thought forms with the mana energy I now have stored within me.

"All the words that I am about to utter will be fixed and engraven in my mind. These words will remain so clear and so fixed in my mind that without being aware of it, my low self and my whole organism will believe the words and will obey them.

"Every day I will be hungry. I will have that pleasant sensation which will make me desire to eat. I will eat with a healthy appetite, but never eat too much. I will know when I have had enough. I will digest my food properly and my body functions will take place in a regular manner. Every night I will fall asleep whenever I wish. My sleep will be calm, peaceful and profound, untroubled by bad dreams or tensions of my body. My dreams will be pleasant ones. Upon wakening, I will feel well, bright, alert and ready for the new day.

"With those things where I have lacked confidence in myself, I will now have abundant confidence. I repeat, I . . now . . have . . confidence. This confidence is based upon the immense power I know I have within me. This power enables me to accomplish any task within my reason. With this confidence I can do anything I wish to do. Whenever I have a task to perform, I will always think of it as an easy job.

"I see myself as a very healthy person, strong and whole. My outlook on life is one of happiness. I see myself as safe, serene and calm . . . happy and well.

"I believe these words with my entire mind and body. I know that they are true. My low self wishes to cooperate with me. I am one with the infinite power of my three levels of mind. All is right . . . so be it."

After a pause of a few moments, tell your low self, "Now, this session of suggestion is over. I want you to stop relaxing and become alert and full of energy."

Imagination plays a far more important role in our lives than most of us realize. A human being always acts and feels and performs in accordance with what he **imagines** to be true about himself and his environment. If a hypnotized subject is told that he is very cold, he will not only shiver and appear to be cold, his body will react as well. Goose bumps appear and thermometer readings have shown that the temperature of the hands and feet will drop. The nervous system cannot tell the difference between an imagined experience and a real experience; it reacts appropriately to what you as a conscious mind think or **imagine** to be true.

Realizing that our actions, feelings and behavior are the result of our own images and beliefs opens a psychologic door to obtain success and happiness. Mental pictures offer us an opportunity to develop desired traits and attitudes. Instead of trying hard by conscious effort and will power to accomplish something, and all the while worrying and picturing all the things that are likely to go wrong, simply picture to yourself the desired end result and your low self will take over.

This technique can help you in personality transformation. You simply form a picture in your imagination of the person you want to be and "see yourself" in the new role. This does not relieve you from effort and work, but your efforts will be used to carry you toward your goal rather than in futile mental conflict, which results when you "try" to be one thing but picture yourself as something else.

Attempting to use effort or will power to change beliefs or cure bad habits has an adverse, rather than a beneficial effect. Dr. Emile Coué emphasized that using effort was the one major reason most people failed when utilizing self-suggestion. "Your suggestions must be made without effort if they are to be effective." Another Coué saying was his Law of Reversed Effort: "When the will and the imagination are in conflict, the imagination invariably wins the day." Our currently held beliefs and habits were formed without effort; so it follows that we must use the same process in forming new beliefs.

Physical relaxation, when practiced daily, brings about an accompanying mental relaxation. A relaxed attitude enables us to more easily control our low self and makes it more receptive to our suggestions. We have previously employed the technique of consciously relaxing the muscles of the body. It often helps to visualize a calm and serene memory from your past.

Let us try another exercise. Sit back comfortably or lie down on your back. Consciously "let go" the various muscle groups. Don't make a big effort, just consciously pay attention to various parts of your body and let go. Close your eyes, stop frowning and let your forehead relax. Ease up on the tension in your jaws. Let your hands, your arms, your shoulders and legs become a little more relaxed. Spend a few minutes on this and then stop paying any attention to your muscles.

Now, pick out a very relaxing picture from your past. Just go back in memory to some relaxing and pleasant scene from your experience. Call up from your subconscious the detailed memory images. Perhaps you are thinking of a peaceful scene at a mountain lake. Remember the little incidental things in the environment. Remember the quiet ripples on the water, the rustling of the leaves. Maybe you chose to remember relaxing in the sun on a beach. How did the warm sand feel against your body. Is there a breeze blowing? Are there seagulls on the beach? The more of these incidental details you can remember and picture to yourself, the more relaxed you will become.

Once you feel very comfortable, repeat the following affirmation: "I fully and freely forgive everyone who may have hurt me in the past. I sincerely wish for them harmony, health, peace and all the blessings of life. I am at peace. I am poised, serene, and calm. I rest in security and in peace. A stillness comes over me and a calm quiets my whole being. I, my low self, and my High Self are as one. We work together as a team. My High Self wants to help me; my low self seeks to cooperate with me. I am one with the infinite power of my three levels of being.

"By day and by night I am prosperous in all my ways. I am surrounded with an abundance of those things I desire. I am becoming more successful every day. It is my right to be successful. I have the right to fully develop and express myself along all lines of meaningful life. I am here to lead an abundant life and to be happy, radiant and free from worry. I therefore have all that is necessary to lead a full, happy life."

In this last exercise you did not consciously re-enforce your thought pictures with mana. Instead you tried to generate as much **emotion** as possible. Strong emotion automatically creates mana. Memories charged with emotion are very easy to recall. The experienced thoughts and pictures sent by the conscious mind to the low self, to be stored away as memories, are made strong and enduring by the mana developed through the emotion of the experience.

This exercise should be practiced for thirty minutes every day. It will build new memories in your subconscious and your low self will build a new image of yourself. After a time you will find yourself acting this new role automatically and spontaneously . . . without trying. Your present feelings and fears are automatic and spontaneous, because of the memories, real and imagined, that your low self has stored away. Once your unwanted memories are replaced with desired ones, you will automatically feel different and effort will be unnecessary. The power of suggestion will work just as automatically upon positive thought and experiences as upon negative ones.

Here are the steps which need to be taken in using self-suggestion:

1. Decide what you are going to suggest.
2. Think about it long and hard to be sure you know just what you want. This solidifies your suggestion.
3. Relax the low self in mind and body.
4. Breathe hard to accumulate extra vital force.
5. Speak the suggestion silently or aloud to your low self.
6. Visualize the suggestion. See yourself in the desired state.
7. Finish by telling the low self that the session is over and that it should stop relaxing.
8. Last and most important, expect the low self to react. **Believe** the suggestion will come about.

In case you, as the middle self, decide to change or cancel a suggestion, do not leave the suggested idea lying about. Think long and hard to picture the idea as cancelled. See it as something no longer wanted. Tell the low self in a regular relaxation-suggestion session that the original suggestion is no longer wanted. Make a mental effort to draw the mana force from the original thought form idea and picture it as cancelled. Do not let your old suggestion worry the low self and cause a mental clutter.

Many people find they get better results if they imagine themselves sitting before a large movie screen. They imagine that they are seeing a motion picture of themselves. Make these pictures as vivid and as detailed as possible. You want your mental thought forms to approximate actual experience as much as possible. Pay attention to small details such as sounds, smells and peripheral objects in your imagined environment.

Once again, finish every session by telling your low self to stop relaxing as the session is over. It is important to take this step, because the point where suggestion begins to work and where it finished is hard to determine. Some people are very suggestible and some are not.

Another important technique in the use of self-suggestion is to use Sleep Suggestion. The mechanism is very simple. Before you go to bed, tell yourself, your subconscious, that you are going to create thought forms, which will remain firmly fixed within your subconscious while you sleep. This technique was presented in 1893 by Thomas J. Hudson in his book, "The Law of Psychic Phenomena." He states: "There is nothing to differentiate between natural sleep and induced sleep. The condition of natural sleep, being the most perfectly passive condition obtainable, is the best condition for the reception of telepathic suggestions by the subconscious mind." In other words, when the middle self is asleep, the low self is wide open to receive suggestion. It is only your conscious middle self that sleeps, and your low self will dwell on your suggestions throughout the night. Sleep Suggestion is an excellent method of setting one's moods for the following day.

Chapter VI

"Effective Prayer"

Self-suggestion is a means of conditioning the subconscious mind to react to the desires of the conscious mind. The most sophisticated form of self-suggestion is not only to obtain the cooperation of your low self, but also to obtain the help of your High Self. This is accomplished through the use of the Huna prayer technique. Many prayers are just empty words, for in most religious practices prayers are little more than a ritual. However, prayer is the central theme in the use of Huna. Huna prayer technique allows the conscious middle self to contact and obtain the cooperation of one's Superconscious, the God within.

All prayers are sent telepathically from the subconscious to the Superconscious. No matter to whom you pray, whether it be to God or Jesus or some other diety, there is only one place where "prayer" can go and that is to the High Self, or as it is called in Hawaiian, the *Aumakua.* In Christianity, we are taught that we pray directly to God. The Huna philosophy tells us we must pray **through the subconscious mind**, or low self, to the Superconscious.

The conscious mind or middle self can think or reason. It is the self that "talks" in order to transmit ideas. The subconscious mind or low self cannot reason. It serves as a memory bank and conveys these memories in the form of sensations or thought pictures. These thought pictures are the basis of telepathy.

Telepathy is the conversation of two people along a "mental telephone wire." If your spouse sends you a telepathic message to bring home a pound of butter, the low self transmits the message in **picture symbols** not in words, for it cannot use words. It gives you a picture of your spouse and follows that with a picture of butter. You do not know how you get the impression, but you know that you get it. You bring home the butter.

An important fundamental belief in the Huna system is that ALL PRAYER IS TELEPATHIC and telepathy is made of messages sent in picture form by the low self. Our middle self gives our prayer first to the low self. It changes our wants into pictured thought forms and sends these thought forms telepathically to the High Self.

If you picture yourself in perfect health and impress that thought on the low self as a desire, it will make a picture of you in perfect health and will send this picture to your High Self. The High Self answers the prayer by "materializing" the picture thought forms for you. This is the secret of secrets in Huna: your picture must not include your sickness. If you pray, "Heal my illness," the low self will make the picture of you in ill health and will send this thought form as your prayer.

In making your prayer you must create a picture of something already accomplished, not of something which is happening or going to happen. You make the picture of the finished fact. Consider the desire as already accomplished, completely and perfectly.

In the 1930's the Frenchman, Dr. Coué, taught this positive picture technique in his invaluable formula: "Every day, in every way, I am *getting* better and better." He pictured the "getting well" process as a thing in the future. A better affirmation would be: "Every day in every way, *I have* perfect health." We must hold this picture of ourselves as perfectly healthy here and now.

The Huna initiates used symbols that are very picturesque. For instance, they used the symbol of "water" for "mana," the vital force. The Hawaiian kahunas used the word *Ho-ano* for "to worship." *Ho* is from *hoo,* the root meaning "to make" and *ano* is "a seed." The kahunas planted a seed with the High Self and sent the vital force, "water," so that it would grow. We cannot send a sufficient supply of vital force with just one prayer to grow the seed to reality on the physical plane. We must contact the Superconscious daily, accumulate an extra supply of the vital force, repeat our prayer, word-for-word as we have memorized it, and send it again with the vital force. This process will strengthen the seed picture and will help the High Self to continue to grow the seed. Once planted, **the seed must not be dug up to see if it is sprouting.** This shows doubt or lack of faith and the roots will be destroyed, stopping the growth of the prayer. If we have no faith, the seed will not take on substance and will not materialize into an actual condition on the physical level.

A most important Hawaiian word is *ano-hou,* the kahuna's word for the "answer" to a prayer. Here once more is the root word for "seed" and with it the root *hou,* which means "to make new or restore" or "to change a form or appearance." *Hou* also means "to pant or breathe heavily," in which we cannot mistake the coded message of the deeper breathing necessary for the accumulation of mana.

The first thing to be done in making a prayer is to decide exactly what one wishes to ask for. One must be very sure to have the exact need properly in mind. The prayer must be such that it will not be changed later on. Imagine yourself as already having the desired thing. Try it on as you would a new suit. See if it fits. Try to see the consequences of your desire, both the good and the bad. You may be praying for a "White Elephant," such as a new car with payments that are too high, or a larger house that will take too much time and energy to maintain.

Let your desire churn over in your mind. Consider it carefully and entirely. If you desire a new suit, consider the color, the style, the way it will look on you. Then drop the thought for a while. Later, think it over again to see if you still want that particular color. Perhaps you really don't want a new suit at all.

To change a prayer once it has been sent to the High Self will jeopardize the results. It is then important to make a very careful prayer to cancel the original desire.

Once you have established the exact picture you wish to create, the next step is to create the mana energy to send with the telepathic message. It is like a radio message that needs electrical energy to be sent out over the air. The low self creates vital force by taking in extra oxygen. Whenever we exercise and need more vital force, we breathe more deeply. We breathe heavier and faster, and we create enough vital force so that we can exert ourselves. A noteworthy part of the Huna concept is that the High Self has a very limited supply of vital force unless it obtains some from the physical body. When the Superconscious is asked to take a pictured prayer to build into a reality, that is to have the prayer answered, vital force must be sent to strengthen the High Self to enable it to produce the desired results.

With the knowledge well in mind of what you will do with your mana, begin to accumulate a surcharge of this energy. Breathe deeper and more slowly. It is most important that you **expect** the low self to accumulate this energy. Tell your low self that you want to generate mana and that you expect it to cooperate in this accumulation. Take breaths in a series of four inhalations and exhalations, pause a moment, and then repeat. This breathing should continue in a slow rhythm until some forty breaths have been taken. The *Ha* Rite of the kahanas means "the forty breath" rite. But the root word *Ha* also means "many," so there is no set number. If you begin to feel dizzy from too much oxygen, slow down or pause for a while and repeat your command to your low self that you are generating mana and expect it to help in the accumulation. All you are doing is furnishing the low self with enough oxygen so that it can burn blood sugar from the liver to manufacture the extra vital force.

Once you have generated a large surplus of mana, you are ready to deliver your prayer to the Superconscious. Repeat the words that describe the thing that you want. As you describe it, you are making a "thought form" picture. The subconscious will receive this "thought form" exactly as you have described it. You then direct your low self to send your prayer to the High Self, so that it may be materialized and made into a reality. You also mentally send the charge of vital force as a gift to strengthen the High Self. Take your time. The important point is to hold the desired picture in your mind and to keep thinking of the low self and the High Self. Your low self will learn very quickly to contact the High Self and to send the thought picture. Once you have sent your desired "thought form" along with the extra gift of mana to the High Self, ask that the picture become a reality on the physical level.

Do not be abrupt when ending your prayer action. Pause a bit, after a while you will come to **feel** what is right. You may wish to use the closing phrase of the ancient kahunas, who said, "My prayer has now taken flight. Let the rain of blessings fall. It is finished." Then you release the subconscious. By doing that you release the Superconscious. If your prayer has been successful and you wait expectantly, you may sense this rain of blessings. It is a return of the mana you have sent. The gift of vital force is somehow converted to an energy level that can be used by the High Self, and it may be returned to cleanse and to bless you. You may actually feel it. It is like a little shower of pins and needles, as from a very sharp shower, falling on your head and shoulders. If you feel nothing, have faith and say, "I have delivered my prayer, and now I leave things in the hands of my High Self, the Superconscious. It is only a matter of time before my desire will materialize."

It is very important to generate as much emotion as possible in desiring the prayed for condition. The low self is the center of the emotions, and if you can desire fervently, you will know that the low self is helping with the prayer. A "cold" prayer is a reasoning action of the middle self, but add the cooperation of the low self and the prayer becomes a "warm" and living emotional desire. An example is the emotional heart cry for "Help" which often reaches the High Self in emergencies. Strong emotion causes the instant giving of what mana we have in the body, and the High Self takes and uses this mana. When one is in great need and cries out emotionally, the low self automatically makes extra vital force and sends the worded picture to the High Self.

We are all familiar with the famous miraculous healings that have occurred at the shrine at Lourdes, France. In most of these cases two important elements have been present. First, the patient has had a deep faith that he will be healed. Second, the patient has been in a highly emotional state. In many cases a good Christian has an open path or connection to his own Superconscious. He may think that he is praying to God or to Jesus or to the Holy Spirit or to the Virgin Mary or some saint, but in every case the prayer can go only to one place and that is to the High Self, and it can go only in one way and that is telepathically.

You do not have to be psychic or have special powers to use this Huna prayer technique effectively. Everyone has the ability to contact his High Self, If you wish to test your ability, try to use the Huna prayer in healing. Try simple ills at first. Cuts, burns and breaks are best to practice on. With daily treatments of mana, a surprising response may occur. You may be a natural healer and not know it. Or, with practice, you may be able to develop definite healing powers. You must be willing to practice a little to teach your low self what it is to do. It must learn to take your pictured prayer and send this picture to your High Self. With practice, your low self will become proficient and after a few successful healings, confidence will be gained. It is most important that you have faith in your ability, faith can make all the difference between successful and unsuccessful prayer.

The first step is to create mana by breathing in sets of four as described earlier. You breathe deeply and slowly and rhythmically. Silently ask your low self to manufacture a large supply of mana. Keep in mind that you are going to use this mana for healing. Also, keep in mind that you are going to ask your low self to call upon your High Self to help in this healing.

When you feel that you have accumulated a large amount of energy, make a mental picture of the patient as in perfect health. Do not picture the hurt or illness, picture only the desired condition. Then mentally call to your High Self. Don't "talk" the picture, this just makes words. The low self and High Self need visualized pictures constructed of mana strengthened thought forms. These pictures are your blue prints of what you wish to be.

With your picture of the healed state in mind, approach your patient and place your fingers lightly on the place which is injured. If this spot cannot be touched, hold your hands a short distance from the body and on either side of the hurt. The low self can project your mana, if you mentally request it to do so. Expect your High Self to aid in your healing and mentally direct the mana charge through your fingers and into the patient. Tell your low self to send this mana energy into the patient in order to effect the healing.

The treatment can last a minute or two and then you can relax and recharge yourself with mana and repeat the treatment. End by giving thanks to your High Self and then to your low self. Afterwards, it is a good idea to wash your hands, and tell yourself that you are washing all the illness down the drain, never to return. This will prevent the possibility of picking up the illness through suggestion.

You can get results quite easily which do not involve someone's help. Prayers that involve the help of other people will take longer. For instance, a prayer for a new home requires the cooperation of several people. This desire may take quite a long time to materialize, because the High Self must obtain the cooperation of the High Selves of all others associated with obtaining the new home. You cannot pray, "Give me that man's house," because the High Self will not act to take the house away from someone else. The High Self will act to bring you in contact with someone who wants to sell his house. If your thought picture described a particular style of house, with a certain floor plan, it may take a long time for your High Self to bring you in contact with the owner of such a house. However, if the desire is great, and if you are consistent in your prayer picture, and if you sincerely believe your High Self is working for you, then you will find the type of house that you want.

Max Freedom Long tells of an experience which will illustrate the effectiveness of Huna prayer:

> "My wife and our partner and I used to live in Hollywood, and I had built a very convenient studio in the backyard. I had my desk and typewriter and mimeograph there and spent many happy hours writing and visiting with my friends and answering my correspondence. Eventually the smog became so unbearable that we decided to move. After much searching, we found a house in Vista that was just the right size for the three of us. Unfortunately, the price was a little higher than we felt we could afford.
>
> "Things remained static for a while until I examined myself carefully to see if I had any subconscious blocks about moving. I discovered that my low self was hanging onto the Hollywood property. It didn't want to give up the studio that I had built. So, I talked to my subconscious like a Dutch Uncle and persuaded it to let loose of the studio, which we loved. We had fifteen days of bad smog at that time and, I'm sure, this helped to convince my low self that it was time to move.
>
> "It was not long until our realtor in Vista called to tell us that the owner had not been able to sell the house and that he had decided to reduce the price to our level. Since the house was in probate, the owner would require the full purchase price in cash. This meant we would have to sell our Hollywood house for cash in time to buy the house in Vista.

"After talking things over, we decided to take things on faith and pray our way out of Hollywood and into Vista. We prayed that the owner would accept our offer, and that before the money came due we would have the full amount in cash.

"Everything worked like clockwork. We put our Hollywood property on the market, and made an offer for the house in Vista. One day we received word that the offer had been accepted. And an hour later our realtor in Hollywood called to tell us he had sold our house and for cash. Everything worked smoothly and we closed the deal in Vista. In short order we were able to move out of Hollywood down to the country where there was no smog, and where we had everything desirable in the way of a home.

"This story serves to illustrate the importance of obtaining the cooperation of your low self in achieving desired results. As long as my low self did not want to give up the studio, it did not send my prayer picture of the new house to my High Self. My prayers were ineffective until I persuaded my low self to "let go." Then, with its cooperation, everything developed quickly and as desired by the conscious mind self. Obviously the thought forms of a house in the country were then sent on to my High Self, so that it could take my gift of mana and create the desired end condition."

To review, once you have accumulated an extra charge of mana, command the low self to contact the High Self and to begin sending your gift of mana. Once this order has been given mentally, the picture of the desired condition is to be visualized as perfectly as possible as having already been acquired. Your prayer has been carefully formulated and memorized and should be spoken aloud, slowly and carefully. The prayer should be simply a description of the desired state as though it had **already** been materialized. This description amounts to an affirmative statement, or an affirmation. You present the thought form "seed" of the **end product**. After a pause, give thanks for the expected answer, and then end your prayer quietly.

Mankind has prayed for centuries, often with little or no results. Men have tried endlessly to explain this failure. They have made sacrifices of all kinds; however, they have not known that what must be given as a sacrificial offering is their vital force. The only meaningful sacrifice to our High Selves is the energy we create by breathing more deeply. It is this mana that we consciously offer with the picture of the desired condition to our High Selves. We furnish the thought-form seed. We water it with mana. The High Self then begins to materialize or grow the seed. Daily, in full confidence and faith, we send our mana and renew our picture. Then, one fine day, we suddenly find our prayer has been answered.

Chapter VII

"Prayer Habits and Techniques"

Learning how to make an effective prayer is the first and continuing interest of a large number of people who have become familiar with Huna. After reading his second book, "The Secret Science Behind Miracles," many people wrote to Mr. Long for help in solving the varied problems which confront all of us. In 1948 Mr. Long organized a group called the Huna Research Associates with members scattered from Australia to England and throughout North America. The research results were reported by letter, and Mr. Long coordinated the information in a bi-monthly bulletin called the "HRA Huna Vistas."

Much of the research and experimentation was centered on telepathic healing and prayer techniques. Several members were simply curious, but many carried out the experiments with real interest. Every six months Mr. Long cleared the membership list of those who had not sent in the requested reports (which were the only means of measuring the group's progress). For the first five years the group averaged a little over 300 members. Some members were gifted with psychic abilities, found they also had excellent telepathic abilities, and soon became proficient in telepathic healing.

By 1953 the work of the HRA's in testing the Huna ideas had progressed to the point where Mr. Long published his third book, "The Secret Science At Work." This report dealt with the HRA's experiments, their results and conclusions. By this time it was apparent that the basic elements of Huna are part of the ancient wisdom found in some proportions in all religions. In fact, since Huna is compatible with all other religious systems, interferring with none, a thorough knowledge of Huna makes possible a greater understanding of all other systems. Mr. Long's purpose had never been to start a "cult." It was simply to help people help themselves and each other through knowledge of the Huna techniques of prayer, and of a way of life such as was taught by many great initiates of the past under an ancient code of secrecy.

Since the publication of "The Secret Science At Work," the Huna Research Associates have grown in number and experience. Members have continued to experiment in groups or alone, and through "Huna Vistas," have reported the many different techniques they have tried and evaluated. After years of gathering evidence, it is clear that most people approach the Huna prayer method with several prayer habits which must be changed.

A basic problem is that ordinary prayer is a hit and miss repetition of set sayings, the voicing of which often becomes a religious duty. The child who is taught the duty of reciting a prayer at bedtime may carry this habit into later life, but it is only an unproductive imitation of the fine art of complete, effective prayer. The correct technique is really very simple once one becomes familiar with the method.

Most of us fall into the habit of hurrying our prayers, causing us to voice only empty words. If prayer is to be effective, it must be made in a slow, orderly fashion with a feeling of strong emotional desire. Unless an individual takes the necessary time to generate this emotion, the prayer will be "flat" and unproductive.

The average person rarely prays with a feeling of emotion. Yet strong emotion guarantees that the low self will be impressed, will generate the mana energy, and will pay attention to the request. When confronted with an urgent need, a person will cry out to God asking for help with a great upsurge of emotion. Where strong emotion is aroused, there is invariably a sudden building up of vital force. In urgent prayer this force is used automatically by the low self to make the telepathic contact with the High Self and to send the empowering flow of mana with the prayer. When making a Huna prayer, you must generate all the emotion you can in desiring the changed condition. The low self controls the emotions, and if you can desire greatly and fervently, you will be assured that the low self is helping with the prayer.

A person will find it impossible to generate the necessary emotion if he lacks deep concentration. (Some may even drift off to sleep during a prayer action.) The will of the middle self directs and controls the making of prayer, and the force of willpower is not exerted unless the conscious mind is alert and concentrating its full attention to direct the low self through each step of the prayer. The fundamental basis of the Huna prayer is the generation of images or thought forms with the mind. Tests carried out by the Huna Research Associates showed that the low self requires effort to focus its attention on a given image. It tires easily and, despite the determination of the middle self, the image may fade and become merely a memory. If the middle self is not alert, the low self will then substitute some other image and start a train of thought more to its liking.

Some HRA's reported an inability to hold a mental image for more than five seconds. Others, especially those who had training in concentration, reported holding an image for up to three minutes. The average was about thirty seconds. Experiments in allowing the mental picture to "move," like a short piece of film, revealed that moving images could be held with ease and the period of concentration extended indefinitely.

Before language was invented, primitive man communicated with his fellow man by drawing crude pictures on the walls of his cave. Later, in Egypt, glyphs or picture writing was used. These pictures were symbolic of some experience, and they would call to mind, through association by the observer, the experience for which the symbols stood. Eventually symbols were combined to represent a whole chain of incidents and finally these became the letters of an alphabet. Like primitive man, modern man can still create mental images. When we describe a condition, we can call upon our memory to produce a picture of the condition. Then as we "see" ourselves experiencing the condition in our mind's eye, we put what we "see" into words. But words are simply sound symbols and as the listener hears the words, he must translate them back into mental pictures in *his* mind in order to "see" the condition.

The low self contains the memories and it communicates these memories through the use of telepathy, or visual pictures. However, any memory of an event or condition will contain, in addition to its appearance, the taste, smell, feel, sound and place in time of the event. A good mental picture of a future condition should be made to contain all these aspects. The eye is the most highly evolved of the senses; so it is natural that visual images are used by the low self as the communication method in telepathy. The ideal way to create thought forms of a prayer condition is to use visual pictures for the framework. To these should be added such other sensory impressions as may be clearly and vividly imagined.

A number of years ago I wanted an exotic sports car which had been built expressly for an auto show. The price was far beyond my means; however, I desired this automobile with all my emotional being. I collected pictures and engineering data on the car. I knew at just what engine speed I should shift the gears. I imagined myself driving the car around a particular curved street in my neighborhood. I could feel myself maneuvering the car around the curves. I could feel the leather seats against my body. I imagined the sound of the engine as it revved up to speed. I could also hear the steady hum of the automobile as it traveled along the highway. I could smell the newness of the paint. I imagined myself waxing the car, shining the chrome, and tuning the engine. In short, I applied every emotional aspect of owning this particular automobile to my desire for it.

Eventually the car was shown at the San Francisco Auto Show and I had a chance to actually touch and sit in it. I told the manufacturer's representative of my desire to own the automobile, gave him my name and telephone number, and asked that he contact me if the price was reduced. After about a month I received a call from him. A man had made a sizable down payment on the car and had then declared bankruptcy; the manufacturer was willing to sell me the car for the balance due. I still needed more money than I had saved; however, the representative's son wanted an automobile similar to the one that I currently owned, and he offered me a sizable trade-in allowance for my car. I could afford the difference and we made the transaction.

This example illustrates the results which can be obtained if one can desire with visual images strengthened by true emotion. The events which led up to my acquiring the automobile could never have been planned. They simply happened, and the end result was the materialization of my prayed-for condition.

A common prayer habit, which must be corrected, is that of describing the problem when voicing the prayer. Instead, the desire must be stated positively. If fears or negative statements are mingled in with the prayer, these are also made into thought forms, along with the positive statements, and are sent to the High Self to become materialized. This problem can be avoided by giving thanks for the answer, as if it had already occurred. Instead of praying for the cure of your aching arthritic hands, give thanks that your High Self made your hands well, comfortable and strong. Incorporate into the prayer the words: "I see." Pray: "I see my hands as well, comfortable and strong." This technique eliminates any tendency to form negative, unwanted thought forms in the prayer. The subconscious mind makes no distinction between constructive and destructive thoughts. It works with the material that you feed it. Your low self cannot reason logically and will send **any** thought form you create to your High Self; so it is important to visualize only those conditions you desire when making your prayer. You must make the mental picture of the thing desired, NOT of the present, unwanted condition.

Jesus advised that we "Ask, believing that ye have received it now." The kahunas likened prayer to the planting of a seed. To them, the full grown plant was already in the seed. When they made a prayer, they thought of the outcome as something already as real as the potential plant within the seed. Time must be allowed for the growth of the plant, but the actual plant is a basic reality. Understanding this, you can think of the desired condition as being already a reality without insulting your reasoning powers.

If you are seeking promotion in your work, imagine your employer, supervisor, or loved ones already congratulating you on your promotion. Make the picture vivid and real. Hear the voice, see the gestures, feel the reality of it. Continue to do this with deep emotional desire and you will experience the joy of answered prayer.

Since one's doubts, fears, and worries will corrupt a prayer, these thoughts must be laid aside before approaching the serenity of the prayer period. The relaxation of body and mind helps in clearing away the worries and fretful mood of the day. A mental or verbal request to the low self to put away all distracting fears or angers is helpful. One effective technique for gaining its attention for this request is to slow the breathing rate down to one inhalation for each six heartbeats and one exhalation for each eight. This also acts to quiet the mind and relax the body. Such soothing of the low and middle self is of lasting value, whether a full prayer is to follow or not.

For effective prayer, it is crucial simply to visualize the desired end result and not be too specific as to how it should be brought about. This leaves the High Self free to bring about the condition in its own way. When the end condition has been imagined, the High Self finds the means for its realization. If we try to anticipate all the steps leading up to the end condition, we may hamper the High Self in its work. We may believe that certain events must occur to cause other events which will result in the desired end condition. However, our High Self is our *Parental* Spirit and knows far more than we; it may decide that an entirely different route should be followed to obtain the desired condition.

A friend once wanted to sell his home. He visualized all the steps necessary to effect the sale. He visualized a buyer knocking on the door and asking to see the house. He saw the buyer looking through the rooms and talking things over with his wife. He then imagined the negotiations over the price and the signing of the contract. All these things came about; however, the bank refused to lend the necessary money to the buyer. My friend then tried simply to imagine the end result. He visualized handing a buyer the deed to his home and saw himself moving away. He did not include any logical steps to effect the sale, simply the end result. It was not long before a real estate agent called to tell him that a client, who had never seen his home, wanted one exactly like it. The buyer was from out of town, handled all the transactions via the telephone, and the only contact my friend had with the buyer was when he transferred the deed.

If you are praying for your own good fortune, you have your own High Self waiting to aid you, but if your request involves others, you may have to enlist the help of their High Selves. The kahunas believed that when a request was made which required the assistance of others, one's High Self would obtain the cooperation of the *Poe Aumakua,* or "Great Company of High Selves," to effect the materialization of the desired condition. They taught that all prayers must first go to the *Aumakua,* the High Self of the individual; however, should the High Self not be able to bring about the request alone, it could carry the prayer to the High Selves of the others involved. Above the level of these High Selves are still higher levels of consciousness which are entirely beyond human conception, but which can create events or conditions on a wider scale.

Decision is one of the most important elements in effecting prayer. Analysis of reports made by many people who have had success with the Huna prayer method disclosed that every one of them had given careful consideration to the desired result. They decided exactly what they wanted and then stuck by their decision. Those HRA's who failed in their prayer results had experienced difficulty in reaching a decision; never committing themselves to a concrete goal.

The "seed" or thought form picture of a desired condition cannot be changed once it has been determined. Once the seed of an oak tree has been planted, it cannot be changed into a maple tree. Once prayer has been offered for a cottage at the beach, it should not be changed to a cabin in the mountains. If you were to enter a taxi and give the driver a half dozen different directions, he would become hopelessly confused and would probably refuse to take you anywhere. Conflicting thought forms will only confuse your low self and will probably cause it to reject all of them. There must be a clear cut idea of your desires in your mind before your prayer will become effective.

The kahunas memorized their prayer chant and then recited the chant three times. They wanted to be certain that the prayer would not be changed. This is a good habit to acquire. Once you decide just what you desire, write your request down and then memorize it. The physical act of writing your request helps to impress the low self and obtain its cooperation. Memorizing the request assures that you will create the same thought form each time you make your prayer.

If you tell others about your decision, be sure that they will be in complete harmony and sympathy with your desires. Close friends and relatives, while not meaning to do so, often handicap one through "opinions" or humorous ridicule, which destroys the confidence. The logical middle self must believe that the decision is possible; for what the middle self cannot logically accept, the low self certainly will not accept. If the low self disbelieves, it may lose all interest in the request and not even bother to send the prayer picture to the High Self. To the kahunas, a prayer had to be "of things possible to obtain," otherwise they were not *pono* or "belonging to the seat of possible thought."

Another point which should be carefully considered before making a request is that the High Self is never party to a theft. It will not "rob Peter to pay Paul," and it will not force anyone to do something against his will. You cannot ask your High Self to "make" someone love you or to take something away from someone and give it to you. In order for a desire to be "right" for you, your low self must believe that it is "right" for all concerned. You must consider the effects of your desire on your relatives, friends, and business associates, if they will be involved.

Many people have a sudden desire for something and immediately make a "give me" type of prayer. They too often find that they have wished upon themselves a white elephant, such as a car with payments that are too high, or a house which is entirely too large. It is imperative to investigate the total consequences of the desire. In order for a request to be "right," it should be for the benefit of all concerned. A man might desire a large house where he could entertain all his friends; however, his wife might find the many rooms too much to clean. A wife might desire an expensive car; however, her husband might not be able to afford the payments. A husband might pray for a new job with better pay, only to find that the added responsibilities require his absence from the home to an extent that his wife and family would be unhappy.

The thoughtful person will take plenty of time to get the prayer picture clearly in mind, including the consequences and obligations. It is best to imagine that the prayer has been answered, and then try it on like a pair of new shoes. See if it is a comfortable situation. Make sure that what you are praying for is truly desired. When it materializes it might entail added responsibilities which, when thought over, are not desirable.

A HRA reported to Mr. Long of his experience when praying for the healing of a young man who had lost the use of his legs through polio. Eventually the useless legs began to tingle and show signs of regaining strength. The young man suddenly became panicked by the prospect of going out and earning a living. He had neglected to try on his desire of having healthy legs with the accompaning obligations of good health. When he finally realized these obligations, his legs again became numb and useless. Obviously both his middle self and his low self were dismayed at the discovery that he was being healed.

Many will assert that the greatest of all riches can be evaluated only in terms of health, friendships, harmonious family and business relationships, and introspective harmony which brings one peace of mind. However, man is on earth to lead a full and abundant life, and this includes acquiring all necessary material needs.

There is absolutely nothing wrong in praying for the material things of life. In the major religions of India, teachings prohibit the desire for material wealth. The religious individual tries to escape from life by ceasing to desire anything. In Christianity there is a doctrine that the ills and poverty of earthly life are to be born with patience and resignation, while every effort should be made to insure a happier life in the hereafter. The kahunas believed it to be right, as well as possible, to have a good and happy life both here and in the hereafter. They concentrated their attention on living the earthly life in the best possible way. We are put on earth to live, to grow, and to progress. The parental High Self wants his children, the low and middle selves of the body, to be happy and free. Money and material things are essential for freedom of the body and mind. Man should, therefore, have all the material things needed to lead a full and prosperous life.

The Biblical words, "Seek ye first the Kingdom of God and all these things shall be added unto you," have been misconstrued. In the ancient lore, the "Kingdom of God," or heaven, is the High Self. "To seek the Kingdom" is to come to a rational belief that there is a High Self and then to cause the low self to contact the High Self to present the prayer picture. Then "all these things," which you can gain through prayer, "will be given unto you."

Once upon a time a man took up the study of magic in hopes of finding a secret formula to enable him to become rich and powerful. Eventually he discovered a manuscript on which was written a magic invocation to seven gods. However, each god had stated certain conditions which must be understood by the suppliant before his requests could be granted. The first god would answer no prayer for something foolish. The second would answer no prayer which asked that something belonging to another be taken away and given to the suppliant. The third god would not aid anyone who thought he was better than anyone else. The fourth would not answer a prayer for someone who already had more than his share of the good things. The fifth god would not grant something not well deserved, and the sixth would punish the suppliant who asked for his own aggrandizement, glory and rise to power. If one was frowned upon by the other six gods, the seventh would drive him from before their faces.

The man anxiously reviewed what he had discovered. He tried to think of a single thing he had meant to ask for which did not violate the limitations set by the gods. He considered his many blessings, finally recognizing that riches and power do not necessarily bring happiness, he slowly burned the manuscript and returned home.

The safest prayer that we can make is for guidance from our parental High Self. To think correctly, scientifically, we must know the "Truth." To know the truth is to be in harmony with the infinite intelligence and the power of our High Self. The middle self of man needs guidance in order to grow mentally and spiritually. We can also ask for guidance in our daily living. Our High Self is our Guardian Angel, protecting and directing us in endless ways. The many things that just "seem to happen" by chance are through the guidance and direction of our High Self. We should consistantly invite It to take an active part in our lives, for we are never really complete until we have all three selves of our body working in total harmony.

In seeking guidance for a particular problem, simply pray for right action. Your course of action will be directed and controlled through the wisdom of your High Self, which is all-wise and omnipotent. The secret of guidance for right action is to devote yourself to the right answer mentally, until you find a response from within. You may not always receive a response right away; however, have faith and **believe** that you have the answer **now**. Feel the joy of the answer and your low self will respond to the feeling. Continue to turn your request for guidance over to your subconscious for transmittal to your Superconscious. In time your answer will come as a feeling, an inner awareness, whereby you **know** that you know.

It is, of course, essential to take all possible steps on the physical plane to help bring about the desired conditions. You cannot serenely fold your hands and wait. "God helps those who help themselves," and the middle self is one of the three partners of living. Each partner must do its utmost to bring about the answer to prayer. Remember, the only way your High Self can communicate with you is through telepathic use of thought forms. These are transmitted through your low self to your middle self in the form of hunches or sudden ideas. These will come automatically, spontaneously, like a bolt from the blue. Follow these hunches, for they are directives from your Superconscious.

Why does a favorite painting or photograph stand out in your memory? Something caught your interest and aroused your feelings to make an impression. Similarly, countless pictures that you have created in your imagination made an impression on you and have been stored away in your memory. The feelings associated with these imagined pictures also influence you. Your conscious mind is like a sieve or a filter in that it rationalizes all your imagined pictures before passing them on to your low self. This is the normal, automatic process; however, the uncontrolled conscious mind of an individual will send all wrong thoughts and feelings to the subconscious along with the good. Unless you stand guard over what you take in, there is no sifting or filtering of the bad from the good. They all go telepathically into the inner consciousness of your low self. What goes in must come out in the form of your future.

The future, which is the result of habitual thinking, is already in your mind. The High Self is able to see what is being made for the future. Conditions are first built into thought forms and then, at the proper time, the event or condition is materialized into its physical form. Every day we create thought forms from our hopes and fears. These thought forms are sent to our High Self and are used to build our future. To change the future, which we have built in this haphazard way, we must send mental pictures of our desired conditions through prayer. Our High Self must then break up the thought form bodies of the unwanted things already created for us in order to replace them with the new. These unwanted conditions sometimes fall upon us, and it often seems that things are getting worse, not better. This important fact **must** be thoroughly understood, because during this period of "breaking up" of the old, we may come to believe that the Huna prayer techniques of positive or creative thinking do not work.

Persistence is an essential factor in the procedure of altering undesirable conditions. The majority of people are ready to give up at the first sign of opposition or misfortune. This weakness can be overcome only with effort. The ease with which lack of persistence may be overcome depends entirely on the intensity of one's desire. Spasmodic or occasional prayer will be of little value. To obtain results, one must develop the **habit** of prayer. The kahuna's term for "to make new" was *hou.* Secondary meanings for this word are "to soak with water" (a symbolic meaning for supplying mana to "water the seed" of the desired condition) and "to repeat any act, to do again," which describes the necessity of repetition of a prayer. A series of prayers, with the unchanged seed picture and mana energy given daily to the High Self, must continue until the harvest appears. Progress may be apparent during the growth period, as in gradual healings; on the other hand, one may reap the harvest quite suddenly, as in acquiring some material desire.

The habits of desire, decision, imagination, emotion, confidence and action lead to effective prayer. Dr. Frank W. Gunsaulus, the educator and clergyman, wanted to organize an educational institution in which young people would be taught to "learn by doing"' He needed a million dollars in order to start this college. One Saturday he realized he had persistently **desired** the money for over two years, but had never really done much about it. He recognized that the time had come for action and decided that he would obtain the necessary million dollars within a week.

The moment he reached a definite **decision** to get the money within a specified time, a strange feeling of assurance overwhelmed him. He suddenly had a wonderful idea; he would preach a sermon entitled: "What I Would Do If I Had a Million Dollars." He announced his topic in the papers and started making notes for the sermon. That night he went to sleep with a feeling of **confidence** for he could actually **imagine** himself *already in possession* of the money. The next morning he was so excited that he forgot his notes; however, when he began his sermon, he closed his eyes and spoke with the **emotion** of his heart and soul. When he had finished, a man made his way to the pulpit and said, "Reverend, I liked your sermon. I believe you can do everything you said you would. To prove it, if you will come to my office tomorrow morning, I will give you the million dollars. My name is Phillip D. Armour." Dr. Gunsaulus did go to Mr. Armour's office and was presented with the million dollars. With the money he founded the Armour Institute of Technology.

"HUNA PRAYER FORMAT"

Following are the elements of a complete and perfect prayer along with suggested affirmations:

1. **Decide exactly what is to be asked in prayer.**

2. **Obtain the cooperation of the three selves:**
   This requires the complete relaxation of the body, the low self and the conscious mind, followed by meditation of the High Self in order to draw it near to you.

3. **Generate a surplus of mana, the life force:**
   I am now going to generate mana by breathing deeply. I am gathering extra mana as I draw in more and more oxygen. I ask my low self to assist me in generating and storing this force. My will is being made strong and enduring so that I am filled with the determination to accomplish these things which I desire.

   Take a series of deep breaths:
   My vitality is building up; my low self is creating mana. Mana is flowing as water into a bowl. Energy is being stored in the bowl. I can see the mana rising higher and higher in the bowl until it overflows.

   Continue the breathing until you feel fully charged:
   I now command my low self to hold this mana energy, until I am ready to send it to the High Self.

4. **Make contact with your High Self:**
   Parental Spirit, who dwells in the realm of Light, I call to you. May the perfection of Your level of being be reflected to my level of being. I ask that You lead and guide me in all that is being done. I ask that You take an active part in my life.

   May Your power create for me the good things, first in Your perfected realm and then cause them to appear as realities on my physical level.

5. **Make the mental picture (thought form) of the desired condition:**
   I now make in my mind the mental picture of that which I desire. I feel a deep, emotional need for this request.

   Repeat your request three times with as much emotion as possible:
   I see myself as already obtaining my request, and give thanks for it.

6. **Send the thought form to your low self to present telepathically to your High Self:**
I hold this picture before the mirror of my High Self and reflect it down into the depths of my low self.

7. **Strengthen the thought form with mana and send it to your High Self:**
I now send this thought form picture along a stream of mana to You. May this gift of mana empower You to work on Your level.

8. **End the prayer with a feeling of faith and confidence:**
I end my prayer and release it to Your keeping to work with as You see fit. I know that is is only a matter of time until my request appears as a reality on the physical level . . . . My prayer has taken flight. Let the Light of my High Self shine back to me. SO BE IT.

Chapter VIII

"The Unanswered Prayer"

Having given the mental picture of your desired condition to your low self, you may be confronted with the problem of whether it has transmitted the picture to your High Self. The low self may either obey your order to deliver the prayer picture, or it may simply drop the thought form into its vast memory storage bank. The problem is threefold: the low self may simply have not paid attention; it may feel that the request is unreasonable; or it may not feel worthy because of guilt feelings.

Mr. Long and the Huna Research Associates found that prayer went unanswered when no emotion of any kind was felt at the moment the High Self should have been receiving the prayed-for image. The low self produces emotional responses, and when there is no emotional reaction of any kind – enthusiasm, doubt, fear or love – the low self is not doing its part in the prayer action. If your low self evidences no emotional reaction toward your prayer, it may not be paying attention to the request. Its attention may wander and turn to other thoughts. You may get a sudden impulse to phone a friend or finish some daily chore.

The HRA's tried many different experiments in their efforts to determine why the low self is sometimes reluctant to cooperate. They discovered that once you decide on the exact thing to be prayed for, you should consult your low self seriously about your decision, explaining the reasons why your desire would be good and right for all concerned. You must convince your low self that what you as a middle self desire will be right for it as well. Relax and invite your subconscious to follow along while you imagine the prayer as answered and the new conditions being enjoyed. Then see how your low self reacts to these new conditions. Little feelings of emotion such as pleasure and contentment or worry and fear will signal its reactions. If there seems to be a negative emotional reaction, wait in a relaxed state. The low self may bring into focus its reason for the disturbed response.

Fortunately, the subconscious can be influenced by argument and reasoning. You must talk to it as you would in explaining things to a child, and slowly bring it around to your way of thinking. The simplest method is through use of the pendulum. Those who have taken time and effort to become well acquainted with their low selves will find they can obtain much information about its beliefs by asking simple questions, which can be answered by "yes" and "no" with the pendulum. Usually the trouble turns out to be some illogical belief of the low self that blocks its desire to help make the prayer.

Following is an actual illustration of this questioning as used by an HRA in reasoning with his low self:

You believe that God can answer prayers, don't

Do you believe that we should pray to God th
No.

You know we have a High Self, don't you? Yes

But you think we should pray only to God? Ye

Is this because we were taught that when we we

Do you believe that we must pray through Jesu

Can you tell the difference between contactin
our High Self? Doubtful.

Of course you can't. All prayers go to the C
were taught to believe in, and that is our Hig
stand? Doubtful.

Then I will explain:

There followed a careful and forceful presen
the High Self is the "Christ Within" for each of
through telepathic images sent by the low self. It
that if the High Self could not answer the pray
request to still Higher Beings, or ultimately, God.

Anyone who has been brought up in the C
find dogmatic beliefs are held by his low self lor
has renounced them. Habits of thought and belief
and the low self may be reluctant to correct de
Often questioning and lecturing must be conti
sessions before the low self is won over to the new

In attempts to alter these unwanted beliefs
the low self places great reliance on the written w
attitudes of thought, which are filed away within
helpful to write down what you realize should be

toward your desire. Written statements plant a detailed picture of the desired belief or objective in your subconscious mind.

There is tremendous power in your spoken or written words, if you really believe what you say or write. Every way that you can express your desire in writing, in speaking, and in mental images helps to keep your thoughts centered upon your target. One excellent visual aid to reinforce a thought form is to write a description of the desire on a small card. Keep it readily available for easy and frequent reference, such as putting the card on the bathroom mirror to be seen every morning after arising and every evening while preparing for bed. Audible repetition also helps to produce results. Tape your desire in the form of a positive declaration or affirmation so that you can play it back. Your low self will then receive the suggestive impact of your own voice.

Some HRA's keep an envelope file containing statements of their objectives in life. These statements are in the form used in self-suggestion; for instance: "I am eating only the right amounts of the right food every day." They reserve certain periods of the day or evening when they can be by themselves to review and reflect upon their written goals. They also take inventory of their progress. You can work on more than one objective at a time as long as they are not in conflict, and you take care to picture them separately. It is best not to offer more than one thought form during a prayer period. If you are working on more than one goal, offer separate prayers with an interval between them. When a goal has been achieved write on the card your thanks to your High Self, and then strive to attain your next desire. It is an endless, satisfying process.

Actions that you have emotionally considered to be sinful will influence your subconscious. Your low self may be ashamed to contact your High Self, because it feels unworthy due to a guilt complex. The complex or fixation of sin was referred to by the kahunas as the "thing eating inside." A conviction held by the low self that an act was sinful may or may not be true; however, once it is fixed in the memory of the subconscious, it is very difficult to remove.

The term "sin" is peculiarly a religious one and implies that man has some relationship to God, or the High Self, which is impaired by the act of "sinning." In Western religions, dogmas teach the concept of sin as an act that goes against the moral teachings of the church or the social customs of the day. If one neglects to attend church services; takes the Lord's name in vain; eats certain foods; or does not perform certain religious duties; or drinks liquor; performs sexual intercourse, gambles or wears certain clothes, then one has "sinned." In Hawaii, the temple kahunas often announced a *kapu,* or tabu, against one action or another. To break this *kapu* was an offense against the temple gods. These *kapus* can be likened to the "sins" of western thought, where social customs and mores have decreed that one must not do certain things, such as smoke, swear, wear lipstick, play cards or go to movies at all or only at certain times and places.

The kahunas did not conceive of sin as it is defined by the moral dogmas of western religions. They considered "sin" as a "hurt" done to oneself or another, when this "hurt" caused a sense of guilt. A barrier is then raised between the sinner and his High Self, so that communication is impossible. The Huna concept of sin revolves around the question of what act may or may not cause the low self to feel guilty and refuse to contact the High Self. The act may not be "wrong" in terms of the reasoning conscious mind, but is, nevertheless, a sin if the subconscious mind feels guilty and ashamed to "show its face" to its High Self. When this occurs, prayer will go unanswered because the desired thought forms will not be transmitted by the low self to the High Self. The basic consequence of sin is the resultant complex or fixation developed within the low self which prevents it from doing its part in the prayer action.

According to the teachings of Huna, an act is wrong only when it is of such a nature as to hurt others, such as physical violence, theft, insult, or other personal injury. Thoughts of hate, greed and envy would, of course, serve to hurt the individual who was filled with these thoughts. Wrongful acts affect others, causing them harm, suffering or loss. Trains of consequences develop, which must be recognized sometime. These consequences are described by the term *Karma.* Karma is nothing more than the moral law: "Whatsoever a man sows, so shall he reap." Thoughts and actions sown by a person will inevitably sometime, somewhere, yield a harvest which returns to the sower. It is not a question of rewards and punishments, but of inevitable consequence. The moral law of Karma is really no different than the physical law every child learns in Physics: "For every action there is an equal and opposite reaction." The natural consequence of a past act must eventually be balanced by a compensating act. This law has nothing to do with sin or justice, it is simply a natural law. Nor does justice, karma, or ultimate retribution have any part in the problem of unanswered prayer.

Jesus said, "If ye were blind, ye would have no sin: But now ye say, 'We see': So your sin exists." This teaching is found in the teachings of the kahunas. The person who hurts others but who feels justified in doing so and who suffers no sense of shame or guilt has not sinned in the Huna sense. His actions will **not** cause his low self to refuse to make contact with his High Self nor will his High Self abandon him. His prayers will be answered. Only an action which causes a complex of guilt within a person's low self is a sin. One's sense of justice only can be maintained by realizing that our Western concept of sin must be changed.

Sin should be determined by one simple test: Does this act cause the individual's low self to feel guilt and thus refuse to contact his High Self in prayer? If it does not, then the person has not sinned.

Only the middle self can sin. Animals kill and eat each other with no feelings of guilt. The animal self of man is the low self, and is therefore incapable of sinning. Being animal, the low self has no inborn sense of right and wrong. (The conscience is simply the natural emotional reaction of a low self which has been taught that certain things are right and others are wrong.) The low self learns these concepts from the middle self, whose reasoning power enables it to know the difference. Because the low self blindly accepts the decisions of the middle self, it will develop fixations of guilt based on the attitudes of the conscious mind. Once a decision is reached that an action is "wrong" and this "wrong" thought form is stored away in the memory, a guilt complex evolves.

A basic human urge is to try to appease a "god" of some kind in order to obtain forgiveness for an act of sin. In most religions, contacting the "god" and requesting a cleansing has grown to be an elaborate ritual. Various cleansing rites have developed which are supposed to make man pure and acceptable before his "god." Primitive religious dogmas taught that a man guilty of sin must please the gods in order to gain their favor. As the primary purpose was atonement, there eventually developed a belief that praise and worship of the gods were necessary to obtain forgiveness. The primitives danced to worship their gods. They fed them burnt offerings such as food, animals and even human sacrifices. Altars were erected as the place of sacrifice and priests were appointed to officiate in making offerings and prayers. From the altar grew the shrine, the temple and the church.

Seeking atonement from sin eventually evolved into a need to attain "salvation." This need arose from a dogmatic belief that man in his normal state was lacking in some way. He might have been "born in sin" or he might have been a member of a tribe that was not of any one "chosen" people. In India, where there was no salvation through a belief in a "savior;" the way led through thousands in incarnations in order to pay off one's karma. Dogmas multiplied as each religion developed. In the eternal search for a means of obtaining an answer to prayer, illogical and strange practices evolved. Flagellation of various forms, abhorrence of sexual relations, circumcision, withdrawal from an interest in life – the list is very long.

This basic urge of religion, the appeasement of gods in order to gain favors, is not found in Huna. The kahunas understood the secret that lay behind the externals of sacrifice. Instead of feeding burnt offerings to the gods, they presented *mana*, the vital life force of the physical body to the High Self so that it could produce results in the physical plane. They did not use temples or shrines. (Spurious kahunas of later times did build temples of lava stone and sometimes offered sacrifices in the vain effort to obtain better results.) The original kahunas used no altar symbols, no incense or other mechanisms. They had no need for "salvation' and they had no belief in a "savior." Their concept of sin was a very simple and workable one. To them, **any** action by a person which caused a complex of guilt within his low self was a sin.

The kahunas used three words in describing the state of severance from the High Self, when caused by the low self's harbored feelings of guilt, shame or fear. These were (1) *ino* which means "to hurt or injure" or "to be wicked;" (2) *hala* which means "to miss the mark or object aimed at" or "to miss the path one should take;" and (3) *hewa* which translates "to be wrong" or "to miss the right path." The "path" and the "way" are symbol words indicating the connection between the low self and the High Self. These same symbols are found in Christianity and the religions of India, but with less direct and definite meanings. Guilt complexes will block the "path" to the High Self. The kahuna symbol for the "open" path to the *Aumakua* was a straight or stretched cord, while a tangled cord (one not pulled tight) was the symbol of the "blocked" path or complex.

When a person had a blocked path, the kahunas performed a ritual of cleansing called the *kala.* The literal meaning of *kala* is "to untie a cord or rope." It also means "to forgive or pardon." The root *ka* means "belonging to" and *la* is "path" and "light" – the Huna symbol for the High Self. The code translation of this phrase is "restoring the Light of the High Self."

There is a significant difference between obtaining forgiveness of sins according to Christianity and the removing of a guilt complex in the Huna system. The Christian believes that his sins are against God as well as man and that he must obtain forgiveness from God. In Huna the High Self is not asked for forgiveness; the sinner has to bring about his own forgiveness by making amends to the person that he has injured. Forgiveness can come only from the individual sinned against, as the High Self cannot be injured in any way. Since the High Self has no part in severing communication between Itself and the low self, it follows that the low self, because of its sense of guilt, is the cause of the blocked path.

If an individual believes he can sin against God and fails to attend church or uses profanity, a fixation of guilt will be established. However, to the kahunas, it was impossible to sin against God, or the *Aumakua.* To hurt God is impossible, for man is far too weak and small to hurt his High Self. The kahunas, knowing that the High Self cannot be injured by mere man, recognized no such thing as a "sin against God."

If one has a feeling of guilt about something done to another person, this guilt may act as a wall between him and his High Self when he tries to reach It in prayer. It is then necessary to convince the middle self that amends have been made before the low self will let go of its belief or feeling of guilt and eliminate the complex. The best remedy is to make amends directly to the one who has been sinned against; however, often it is impossible to go to the person we have hurt. In such cases one can make amends through acts of kindness to others. He can search out those who need help and perform the physical act of helping by giving of his time or money.

The physical stimulus is important. The low self is accustomed to mental activity, but an impression is made by the general physical stimulus through forms of self-denial, such as fasting, stopping smoking or giving something away that the low self feels is valuable. One must not expect either thanks or reward. Once the rational middle self is convinced it has made amends, the low self will normally also feel that good has been done to balance the former wrong of hurt, and it will feel worthy of contacting the High Self.

You cannot hold a grudge or hate another and maintain communication with your High Self. Jesus taught us to pray: "Forgive us our trespasses, **as we forgive** those who trespass against us." Forgiveness of others is necessary to obtain close cooperation of your conscious and subconscious minds. The essential ingredient in the art of forgiveness is the **willingness** to forgive. You must sincerely desire to forgive before the low self will rid itself of its feelings of hate, jealousy, resentment or fear. As long as you entertain negative reactions from your subconscious, (unless you can forgive others) you are actually punishing yourself, for you must release all condemnation, resentment and anger against another before you can obtain creative results through prayer.

You are not being magnanimous when you forgive; you are really being selfish, because what you wish for another, you are actually wishing for yourself – you are thinking and feeling the wish, and "as you think and feel; so are you."

To forgive another does not necessarily mean that you must like or associate with him. You cannot be compelled to like someone; however, you can love people without liking them. Love means that you wish for the other health, happiness and all the blessings of life. The most difficult test of attaining complete forgiveness is thinking well of those who have injured us. If you hear something wonderful about a person who has wronged you and become envious or angered at the news, you have not truly forgiven that person. The roots of hatred are still within your low self. You must continue to pour out love and goodwill, until such time as you meet the person in your mind and find that you are at peace with him.

You may find that it is necessary to forgive yourself. If you have harmed someone, you may feel that God should punish you for your act. This guilt complex is a result of a false concept. God, or your High Self, holds no grudge against you. It never condemns or judges or punishes you. You do this yourself by negative thinking and self-condemnation. Resentment, hatred and hostility are the cause of many maladies ranging from arthritis to cardiac disease and psychosomatic disorders of all kinds. You must forgive yourself and everyone who has ever hurt you in order to have health, peace of mind, and full integration between your three selves.

A simple technique for effecting forgiveness is to quiet your mind, relax and then affirm: "I fully and freely forgive (the name of the offender). I release him/her and completely forgive everything connected with the matter. I am free and he/she is free, and I wish for everyone health, happiness, peace, and all the blessings of life. I do this freely and with my entire being. Whenever I think of anyone who has hurt me, I will say, 'Peace be to you.' " Affirm this as often as the thought enters your mind. You will find that soon the thought of the person or experience will return to you less and less often, until it fades into nothingness.

When the low self believes the person has "sinned," it may punish the person for the sin through an illness or an accident. This can be illustrated by the case of a young man brought up under very strict religious training who refused to enter the ministry and took a job in a furniture factory. The paint and varnish fumes sickened him, so he was transferred to the woodworking department. There the sawdust gave him asthma. He went from job to job; however, some aspect always caused an allergy. Through psychotherapy, he discovered that his subconscious held a deep sense of guilt for his rejection of training for the ministry. Although he had consciously forgotten the memory of this act, the memory remained within his low self as a complex of sin. As he had been taught that all sins were punished by God, his low self caused a dislike, which amounted to an illness, for every occupation he chose. His psychoanalyst forced the young man logically to evaluate his refusal to enter the ministry, yet he remained convinced that he had been guilty of a terrible sin of omission. Eventually he entered a school for ministers and all his illnesses vanished.

In this case the complex was not removed. Since the guilt feelings were held by the middle self as well as the low self, logic and reason did not remove the complex. The middle self must free itself from the idea of guilt before any progress can be made with the low self.

The kahunas believed that removing the "thing eating inside," the complex of guilt, required a combination of logical appeal to the patient's conscious self, suggestion to the subconscious, and a physical stimulus to accompany the ministering of suggestion. The low self is best impressed by real and tangible things, such as the water that is used in many religions to "wash away sins." The kahunas often used water in ceremonial washing of their patient, while giving the spoken suggestion that the sins were being washed away.

While living in Hawaii, Mr. Long knew a healthy and charming Hawaiian who had an affair with another woman, even though he remained devoted to his wife. He caught a cold which soon developed into influenza. Despite excellent medical care, he grew weaker and weaker. After being told that her husband could not live more than a few days, his wife contacted one of the few remaining kahunas who were still alive in Honolulu in 1926.

The old kahuna rubbed the sick husband's body, chanting in a low voice how he was pouring mana energy into the man to make his body strong. After a while, the kahuna began questioning him, asking what he might have done to hurt someone. At first he was met by stubborn silence, but finally the infidelity was confessed. The kahuna then told his wife very simply that her husband had "sinned" against her and was dying because he could not face her. The wife was enraged for a moment but, facing the danger of death to her husband, agreed to forgive him.

Taking a brush of green sword-like *ti* leaves and a bowl of warm water, the kahuna told the patient that because his wife, who had been hurt, had forgiven him, his sins could now be washed away with the water in the bowl. He sprinkled the man's body then brushed vigorously with the leaves, all the while carefully describing how the sin was being dissolved in the water to be washed away. After wringing the water back into the bowl, he asked that the patient watch while the water carrying his sin was poured onto the ground to be disposed of forever.

The patient was then dried and told that his strength was rapidly returning and that he would soon be hungry, would eat, and after sleep would be on the way to recovery. When he awoke hours later, the man asked for more food and was sitting up happily talking with his wife when the white doctor called. After a careful examination of his patient, the knowledgeable doctor asked the wife if she had seen "the other kind of doctor." She nodded, and he went out shaking his head wonderingly.

In this example, the Hawaiian had sinned by the hurt caused by being unfaithful to his wife. To convince his reasoning middle self that he had been forgiven, his wife actually had to speak the words of forgiveness.

This, plus the physical stimulus of the "washing away" of the sin, impressed the low self, which had brought on the illness as punishment for the sin. The complex was removed and, as there was no longer a need for punishment, the man became well.

It is not necessary to find a hidden guilt complex and remove it in order to obtain effective prayer. Since the major cause of unanswered prayer is the reluctance of the low self to play its part in the prayer action, it is more important to simply convince the low self that amends have been made for the hurt done to another and that it is worthy of contacting the High Self and asking for better conditions through prayer.

Chapter IX

"The Significance of Life"

Although Huna is basically a philosophy of life, it is difficult to classify, because it includes at least three poorly defined and inadequately developed sciences. Religion, although it does not have scientific standing, is really the science of the relationship between man and any beings more evolved than himself who may have an influence on his life–either now or in the hereafter. Psychology is a science of the human mind, and Psychic Science, while still in its infancy, is a science based upon considering man as a conscious being who lives in a physical body during a period of earthly life and, after so-called "death," lives in a different "spirit" body.

The religions of the world began with the worship of those threatening aspects of nature–the wind, the sun, fire and water. Spirits of animal and human dead were very much a part of early religions, and vast rituals of appeasement grew by degrees to prevent these spirits from causing misfortune for the living.

Psychic Science or Mysticism has always been integral to religious thought. No century has been without its mediums or psychics who have seen and spoken with the spirits of the departed. Truth became mixed with superstition; however, it cannot be denied that some of these superstitions must be based on actual experience. So much first hand phenomena, confirmed by independent evidence, should not go unregarded especially since rational explanations are difficult to find except in terms of psychic hypotheses. It may be possible to explain an individual case by alleging hallucination, fraud, hysteria, or just plain lying; but it is difficult to explain the sum total in this way. There cannot be so much smoke without some fire. It is not possible that the dread of the magician or witch doctor of antiquity could have arisen without some basis in experience. Forged bank notes would never gain currency unless there were such things as genuine bank notes. It would never occur to anyone to produce fraudulent psychic phenomena unless there had been some genuine basis for the forgery.

For the most part, men of the material sciences have remained blind to what we now call the science of mind, or psychology. Man has been measured in every respect except his mind, for no one could measure the mind in terms of a tape, a scale or a test tube. Only a few years ago, when the subconscious mind was first postulated, the majority of scientists refused to consider the idea. One famous professor at Harvard voiced the opinion of the majority when he exclaimed: "The story of the subconscious can be told in three words: there is none."

Although we now accept the proofs so far discovered through the Science of Psychology, the idea of **survival** of the consciousness, or mind, is far more difficult to prove. In 1967, Mr. James Kidd's estate, valued at $233,000. was left to anyone who could give scientific proof that there was a soul and that it survived death. During the trial in Phoenix, Arizona many individuals and organizations hired lawyers and brought a ponderous amount of evidence before the court. However, no one could come into court with a soul sealed in a test tube and demonstrate its death and return to life. After a lengthy trial, the legacy was awarded to the Barrows Neurological Institute, located in Phoenix, who based their claim on the fact that they were trying to prove the possibility of survival of the soul.

We now know that the physical body is not the grossly material organism we once thought it was. Only a few years ago, scientists thought that the so called "soul" was a part of the human body and died along with it. The body is now referred to as nothing but an electro-chemical machine, and many scientists have concluded that intelligence – consciousness – may not be a part of the body at all, but that it simply manifests itself **through** the body. One may make the assumption that when the body machine dies, the mind will necessarily die as well. But it is equally possible, assuming the mind's independent status, that when mind, or consciousness, leaves a body machine (which it has kept alive by reason of its intimate association with it) that body will then die. If this is so, you (as a unit of consciousness) are simply a temporary tenant living in a complex machine of flesh, gaining experience and evolving through this life experience, finally to depart when the machine has outworn its usefulness.

However, if it *is* true that man perishes with the death of his body, we must live in a world which is fundamentally unjust to many people. Some human beings come into this life with major handicaps. They have to contend with physical deformity, poverty, suffering, cruelty and discouragement. Others, through no merit or effort on their part, are favored with fortune. Philosophically this problem is insolvable if mankind is bounded by this life alone. However, if we postulate that souls or units of consciousness have pre-existed their present incarnation, and that when re-born bring with them the weaknesses and strengths acquired by living prior lives, we can suppose that inequalities and apparent injustices arise from these past lives. We can see that the world is not unjust when we understand that this earthly experience is simply a part of a greater whole which stretches out beyond the portals of birth and death.

The question of rebirth is rather strange to most people of Western Civilization. However, in the East this concept is a way of life. Buddhists and Hindus take for granted that life after life is a normal occurrence. They believe that the human consciousness is committed to an indefinite round of births and deaths until it finally attains its divine nature. There are other forms of this doctrine such as the belief that the soul may retrogress back into an animal form, the transmigration of souls, as the result of a sinful life.

Reincarnation was considered as an integral part of the early Christian teachings, whereby reincarnation corresponded to the Christian idea of purgatory. Since the beginning of the Middle Ages it has been excluded from the majority of Christian dogmas. However, to millions of people, the soul is considered to be something enduring, gaining wisdom by living in various periods of history and in a variety of situations. This idea is not unreasonable, for what the soul, or consciousness, has done once, it could certainly do again. As you develop your awareness you will become cognizant of an increasingly positive conviction that "this life is not all;" that it is part of a continuously unfolding experience.

Science now thinks of man's consciousness as a level of energy. If this is so, it seems reasonable that this energy could be graphically displayed in the same mode as all other forms of energy: by a sine curve. A sine curve is one that rises above a horizontal base and then drops below the base line. All modes of energy demonstrate a continual fluctuation between extreme values which are usually measured as above or below a horizontal base line. A familiar example is the oscilloscope which is used in recording wave forms of energy on a fluorescent screen. It is difficult to conceive that life energy should differ from all other energy forms and that it should not oscillate or pass from one state called "life" to another called "death" and back again.

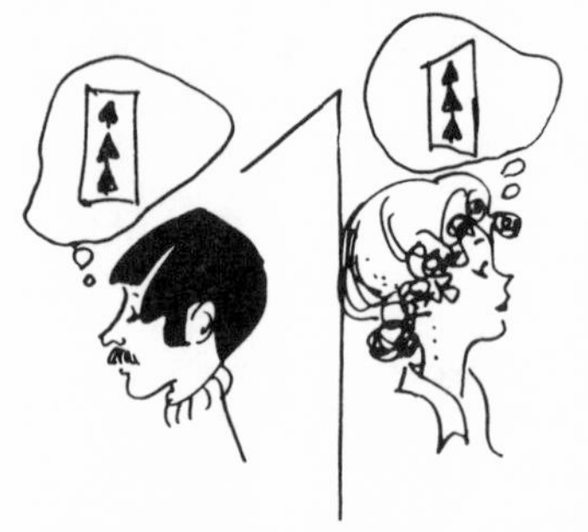

Telepathy, the communication between minds without the use of the senses, has been established as a fact. Dr. Joseph B. Rhine of Duke University has done more than any other one man to make telepathy scientifically acceptable and extrasensory perception a recognized part of the Science of Psychology. When one dies or the mind becomes discarnate telepathy still exists, and so we have the possibility of acquiring knowledge of life after death. There are many stories of mediums communicating with the dead, and there is a large amount of well attested documentation pertaining to this phenomenon. Communications with those entities who have passed to the other side of the sine curve have established sufficient data to accept the possibility that intelligence continues after the physical body dies.

In the Bible we read of the Day of Judgment. This subject has held the fascination of believers for centuries, and they have combed the Prophecies looking for signs of the Last Day. The Indian concept may be closer to the truth. The Vedic lore of India teaches that the soul is tied to a never-ending series of lives. There is a long cycle of outpouring and then a turn in the opposite direction, when the outpouring becomes an ingoing as each cycle ends. Some believe that the fabled Atlantis rose to be a great civilization, then destroyed itself, leaving the world populated by a few pockets of isolated people who began again. This is an interesting speculation that suggests that we may be growing to the close of a cycle, and what the Vedas speak of as the "Long Night" may follow.

However, the human consciousness is actually a unit of energy, and energy can neither be created nor destroyed. No matter what should happen to this infinitesimal speck of dust within the universe that we call the earth, the soul, or self, or mind that is the basis for life on earth must continue to exist.

During life we manifest a web of relationships with other people's lives. Some of these may have deep significance. Occasionally we meet a person who is immediately loved or hated, and we may be dealing with a relationship which pre-existed in a previous life. Love and hate are energies which draw us again and again into interacting orbits.

Many people have memories that, after investigation, can only be memories of former lives. We have all experienced feelings of "having been here before" or "having done this once." In the past decade hypnotic regression into past lives has become a medical tool for psychiatrists in endeavoring to unfathom deep seated mental or physical ills. The recollections are usually very vague, but often fragments from a previous life will be recalled, including the fears and fixations developed in that life. Dr. Kelsey, a psychiatrist, points out many examples in "Many Lifetimes." Evidence is gradually mounting to prove that many people can recall, either naturally or under hypnosis, their past lives. The medium, Geraldine Cummins writes in her book "Perceptive Healing" of going back into the past life of a man who had a fixation which prevented him from signing papers of any kind. She discovered that in the just previous life he had had his hands cut off in connection with signing some papers and had carried over the terror of the experience into his present life. The examples are many. The foremost investigator of this kind of phenomena in the United States is Dr. Ian Stevenson of the Department of Psychiatry and Neurology at the University of Virginia's School of Medicine. Dr. Stevenson analyzed many cases of Indian children having memories of former lives and surroundings. The rebirth was so soon after the previous death that the memory data could be checked. In 1960 he reported in the "Journal of the American Society for Psychical Research" that in most cases the life that was remembered was lived in a different native village, and that there was evidence that the child recalling the memories had no possible access to the particular locality. The detail remembered was quite remarkable.

The case for survival does not rest upon a few examples, but upon many lines of converging evidence. Conclusive proof may be impossible, but such proof is rarely possible in any field of scientific inquiry. There is a vast amount of well-attested data which makes man's survival of death seem highly probable. Some people are in a fortunate position. They can say with complete conviction, "I **know** that I will survive death. I need no evidence to support my knowledge; I have an intuitive certainty." Most people need to form a judgment on such evidence as is available. If we can be satisfied with the **reasonableness** of such a position then, although conclusive proof may be impossible, we may come to accept it as a probability.

The English and American Societies for Psychical Research have reported on many psychic experiments and occurrences since the last century. One of the most interesting cases, recorded in Nandor Fodor's "Encyclopaedia of Psychic Science," involves a Carlo Mirabelli. Born of Italian parentage in 1889 in Sao Paulo, Brazil, his activities are perhaps the best certified in the history of investigations by the Psychical Research Societies. When being investigated in Italy under test conditions, Mirabelli produced messages from many dead celebrities, including 14 pages in Japanese by Muri Ka Ksi on the Japanese-Russian War. In broad daylight, being watched by experienced investigators, Mirabelli often caused dead people to materialize so fully that doctors could take their temperatures. Doctor Fodor describes the materialization of a Bishop Jose de Carmago Barros as follows:

> "A sweet smell of roses filled the room. The medium (Mirabelli) went into a trance. A fine mist was seen within the circle. The mist parted and the Bishop materialized with all his robes and insignia of office. He called his own name. Dr. de Sousa stepped up to him. He palpated the body, touched his teeth, tested his saliva, listened to his heartbeat, investigated the workings of his intestines, nails and eyes, without finding anything amiss. The other attending persons convinced themselves of the reality of the apparition. The Bishop smilingly bent over Mirabelli and looked at him silently. Then he slowly dematerialized."

From time to time there are prodigies born whose knowledge and skill cannot be explained by anything they have learned or been taught. If we accept the possibility of a previous life, we can explain these prodigies as an example of an overflowing of a previously attained ability into a succeeding life. The subconscious, which has stored the memories and skills of the past, influences the new personality. The child prodigy is the reincarnation of a unit of consciousness with a very specialized development. It is sometimes found that the genius fades out at an early age. Other fields of interest are introduced and the exceptional one is withdrawn for the sake of a wider and more balanced development.

The logic of reincarnation is perhaps somewhat like that of education. It is of little use to attempt college until a sufficient standard of achievement has been attained in high school. College would otherwise be a waste of time. It seems that certain important and necessary qualities can only be acquired within the limitations and restrictions of a physical body. We can learn courage only through facing "life" where events are uncertain. Kindness and compassion are also achieved through living a physical, earthly life. There seems to be no definite answer as to the number of times one reincarnates. As in the process of scholastic education, it seems to be up to the individual. A person who learns well from each lifetime of experience will graduate faster than one who learns more slowly.

The ninety or so chemical elements are all constructed from the fundamental particles of matter: the electrons, protons and neutrons. Each of these chemical atoms has varying properties or qualities, none of which are present in the fundamental particles. Combined atoms create molecules, which possess qualities not found in the molecules which compose the cells. Greater wholes are always more significant than the sum of the parts. This is also true in the process of evolution.

Man, as a unit of conscious energy, through an evolutionary process has learned to build a body with which to house his sense of self. After evolving through the mineral phase of existence, man's unit of consciousness entered the vegetable kingdom. Then, always growing and learning, this life energy ran the gamut of experience from fish to bird, and then graduated by a series of incarnations as various species of animal to an incarnation as a member of *Homo sapiens.*

During this process of evolution, something called *intuition* controlled this life energy. Intuition in some way directs life forms of energy. It taught the coral to make a shell from the lime of the sea water; it taught the bird to build a nest and to migrate. Eventually life energy evolved to a point where it no longer depended upon intuition. It could produce a body machine capable of housing a human type of consciousness with the power to use inductive reasoning. Man, as a conscious middle self, separate and distinct from pure animal, had evolved. According to Huna, the animal low self consciousness joins a middle self at this point. This middle, or more evolved, self uses the higher or inductive type of reason.

During the first few lifetimes as a human being, the whole personality incarnates; so the entity is likely to maintain approximately the same capacities and perceptions developed in the previous life. The low self of man stores the memories of the individual lives, and as consciousness evolves the individual "learns." If one is an "old soul," or one who has lived several lives, there are certain things which one automatically "knows." We tend to avoid making the same elementary mistakes again and again. This explains why people are so different. Having had different experiences, they will react differently in a situation according to their recalled inner experience.

Throughout this growth period the High Self is acting as a guide and director. It is the Self which has evolved a step beyond the middle self. It watches over us, never encroaching on our free will, but helping us to gain experience and to grow. The kahunas believed in layers and layers of rising consciousness, but they were primarily concerned with the next level of evolution above the middle self – the High Self or *Aumakua.*

During the earthly period of evolution, the unit of conscious energy we call *man* has a primary task of learning to guide and control the animal, low self part of his makeup. The "young soul" is given to following his emotions (governed by the low self) to direct his life. As one grows older in terms of incarnations, one tends to control the emotions instead of letting them control him. The "young soul" flies into a rage when crossed; the "old soul" overcomes his emotions and endures in silence without resentment.

One emotion that is not overcome is that of love. Love is the common denominator of mankind's evolutionary growth. A perfect capacity to love marks the advanced soul. Eventually one learns to love well enough to evolve or graduate to the level of the High Self. It may take a dozen incarnations for the low self of a person to be less like an animal and more like a middle self, but when the lesson is learned the low self is next born in a body as a middle self. At this point a male middle self steps up to the High Self level where it joins its "soul mate" (the middle self of a female) and the blended and united pair become a new High Self. As a High Self, love becomes perfected and selfless, as does the love of the man and woman who unite and blend their being when they become a new High Self. This is the "marriage made in heaven" which we read in the Bible, and is probably the origin of the concept of "soul mates."

The two-volume work of Gerald Massey, "Egypt, the Light of the World," discusses the cult of Osiris which flourished during the first writings of the Egyptians about 6,000 years ago and absorbed many Huna concepts. Massey shows with elaborate studies that the Egyptians, upon death, went through a series of tests until they finally were united with their soul mates and were given the "robe of glory" to become a High Self. Massey is not specific as to just when and how the final union of the male and female souls is managed; however, he has gone to great lengths to give quotations from the "Book of the Dead" and other early writings, which show very clearly this "marriage made in heaven." The following is one example:

> With Egyptians the soul was of both sexes. The divine being as Ptah and Osiris was of a biune nature. Hence Ptah and Osiris are portrayed as male and female in one image, and the prototype soul, was discreted (distinct or separate) as human in the two sexes. In passing through Amenta (heaven) the human soul is represented as the male accompanied by the female. This soul, divided into the two halves of sex, was united again in establishing an eternal soul. The soul was (originally) divided into Shu and Tefnut (Adam and Eve, the typical two sexes of the Hebrew legend). Adam was *Atum* in the original myths . . . (and) was the lion as representative of the soul or life force . . . Tefnut (Eve) was depicted as the hinder half of the lion with Shu (Adam) as the forepart. The soul that lived forever was held to be established for eternity by the female being blended with the male.

Max Freedom Long points out that the Sphinx was actually a monument to this "graduation," when after the final incarnation and blending takes place the two middle selves evolve or graduate to become an *Aumakua* or High Self. In Christian literature, we have the "Father," but no "Mother," for the Mother was blended into the Father. Massey continues:

> In Africa, Melanesia and other parts, the women will volunteer to be strangled at the funeral of their husbands, or buried alive in their graves. In India it was the custom for the wife to mount the funeral pyre and allow herself to be burned with the husband.

From this we can see how basic Huna truths have become warped as they became half-known. By dying with her husband, the wife is supposed to partake in an eternal soul.

It is evident that the Hebrews carried Huna with them when they left Egypt, for we find coded references to the ancient system in the Old

Testament. In the creation myth of Genesis, man was not merely the crown of the animal world, he was different in an important inner way from any other creature. We read: "God breathed into his nostrils the breath of life and man became a living soul." Man was given a status conferred by some additional factor above the animal: the possession of a middle self within his inner nature. We also find in the story of Adam and Eve the separation of the sexes to give us man and woman.

The sexes reunite at the end of a period of evolutionary growth to become the Superconscious or High Self. The new High Self becomes the Father-Mother of the old low self, which in its turn steps up to the level of a middle self. A new low self evolves from the animal level to form the third member of the new triune man. Think of all three selves of a man incarnating as a team. When one of the team steps up a rung on the ladder of life, the others step up as well always at the same time, never separately. The team is never broken. At the top of the ladder the High Self evolves to an even higher level called the *Akua Aumakuas,* the High Self gods. There are probably many additional levels of evolvment; however, these are beyond the mental grasp of the middle self man for Ultimate God is something which we cannot imagine. When a person steps up a rung, this leaves the lowest rung empty. According to Huna an animal entity is added to the team as a new low self, and the next series of incarnations begin. This belief is illustrated by totem images found from the Eskimos of the Arctic Circle to the aborigines of Australia.

Of particular interest is the classical form of the totem pole found in New Zealand up to modern times. This totem pole represents the belief that man has three spirits, the most advanced of which is a dual entity made up of a combined male and female unit. The lowest figure of the carved pole is a large representative of some form of animal. Above the animal spirit, and often with legs and arms folded around the lower spirit's neck, is a more human figure. Above the second spirit, often with a small body, is a figure with two faces placed back to back on a single head. This top spirit is often depicted with wings which is indicative of a spirit which can fly above the bottom two spirits. The High Self of man does not live within the human body along with the lower two selves (depicted with entwined bodies) but lives "above" the body.

The Hawaiian kahunas considered reincarnation such a commonplace truth that they made no effort to conceal it with a code word. They simply called it *"hou-ola." Ola* means "life" and *hou* means "new; to repeat; to do over again as before." Their phrase *ola honua* translates a "preceeding life" also "naturally, without cause." It is obvious that the kahunas believed it natural and without special cause that men lived through several incarnations before graduating up the ladder of life.

In living as a low self in an animal body, we seem to exist under some set law of growth and evolution, and as middle selves we share the trials and tribulations of the physical body. We are subject to disease and poverty, as well as hurts done to us by the ruthless. Once the body is fatigued, we go to the other side for a while and rest, to absorb the lessons we have learned, and then return to incarnate once again under some great law which guides all of evolution.

For those individuals who are searching for the meaning of life, there is in Huna a splendid purpose behind living. Huna not only offers something which is reasonable and in keeping with the modern theories of evolution, but also gives us a God as something brought down to within our reach. From any point of view, the High Self stands as the most logical and believable concept of "the God that is within us." Above the High Self may be still higher beings, but for the purpose of daily living it is enough to know that there **is** a High Self, that It is a part of our total being, and that It is ready and willing to aid us.

The most important reward gained from the knowledge of Huna is to become aware of the proper means of communication with our High Self. This secret psychology offers the only workable approach to creative thought – that of praying **through** the low self to reach the High Self. The Huna concept of prayer is unique in the field of positive thinking. The only feasible means of obtaining answers to our prayers is to create visual pictures, strengthened with mana created from the **emotion** of desire, and then sending these thought forms (by telepathic means) through the low self to the High Self. One **cannot** pray directly to God. We obtain results **only** by obtaining the cooperation of our subconscious mind in contacting our personal guide through life, our *Aumakua.*

Huna also presents a realistic approach to the concept of sin – that of knowingly hurting another. Thus sin becomes a personal act and is completely independent from the social mores of a particular culture.

Finally, Huna offers a "salvation" or ultimate goal to strive for: that of learning or evolving as rapidly as possible from earthly experiences, while receiving guidance from our High Self. Salvation as a goal is common to all religions; the salvation offered in Huna is to learn to know the High Self and to contact and work with It. Divine Salvation comes after a number of earthly incarnations when the middle self graduates to the level of the High Self. This graduation occurs only when one has learned, as a middle self, to be one with the High Self – to be loving in all things.

BIBLIOGRAPHY

The Works of Max Freedom Long:

Recovering the Ancient Magic (1936, 1978)
Introduction to Huna (1948, 1975)
The Secret Science Behind Miracles (1948, 1954)
The Secret Science at Work (1953)
Growing into Light (1955)
Self-Suggestion (1958)
Psychometric Analysis (1959)
The Huna Code in Religions (1965)
How Everything Was Made (1967)
Mana, or Vital Force (1949, 1976)
Short Talks on Huna (1978)
Tarot Card Symbology (1968, 1972)
HRA Bulletins (1948-1958)
Huna Vistas (1959-1970)
What Jesus Taught in Secret (1970, 1983)

Other Books Related to Huna:

Andrews, Lorrin, **A Dictionary of the Hawaiian Language** (1865, 1974)
Glover, William R., **Huna: The Ancient Religion of Positive Thinking** (1979, 1983)
Hickey, Isabel M., **It is ALL Right!** (1976)
Hoffman, Enid, **Huna: A Beginner's Guide** (1976, 1981)
Huna Research, **Huna Vistas Newsletter** (1973-1981)
Huna Research, **The Huna Work** (quarterly bulletin)
Melville, Leinani, **Children of the Rainbow** (1969)
Nau, Erika, **Self-Awareness Through Huna** (1981)
Rodman, Julius S., **The Kahuna Sorcerers of Hawaii** (1979)
Steiger, Brad, **Kahuna Magic** (1971, 1981)
Westlake, Aubrey T., **The Pattern of Health** (1961)
Wingo, E. Otha, **Letters on Huna** (1973, 1981)
Wingo, E. Otha, **Story of the Huna Work** (1981)

For information on membership,
courses and tapes, write:

Huna Research, Inc., 126 Camellia Drive, Cape Girardeau, MO 63701 USA
Dr. E. Otha Wingo, Director (314) 334-3478